THE FLOWING SAND

THE FLOWING SAND

NO ONE IS SAFE IN A WORLD FULL OF EVIL

Jon Garcia

Palmetto Publishing Group
Charleston, SC

The Flowing Sand
Copyright © 2018 by Jon Garcia
All rights reserved

This is a work of fiction. All characters, organizations, towns, and events portrayed in this novel are either products of the authors imagination or are used factiously. Any resemblance to actual events or places or persons living or dead, is entirely coincidental.

First Edition
Printed in the United States

ISBN-13: 978-1-64111-252-9
ISBN-10: 1-64111-252-2

Dedicated to my brother "Emmy" who I love and miss very much, R.I.P. To Jesus Camacho who was like another brother to me and who always wanted to hear and read my stories, particularly this book. R.I.P, I'm sorry that it wasn't finished before your passing. To all the victims of crime, kidnappings, sex trafficking, physical violence, murder. And last but not least, for all the people who said or never thought it would be completed. Here it is, all twenty-seven thousand one hundred and eighty-two words. :) Enjoy!

ACKNOWLEDGMENTS

I WOULD LIKE TO take this time and thank those who have supported me and been behind me every step of the way. To the ones who read it before hand and encouraged me to go through with getting it published (Conchis, Sharell, and Cesar)! Thank you all so much. I've always said the good thing about writing a story is that you are the creator of everything that happens. Like painting or architecture, you start with a blank slate and build from there. When the building process is complete and you admire the ending of your work you can say I did that, others can say what they could or would have done differently, but it ended just the way that YOU wanted, and that's what counts. My goal for this story was to open the eyes of parents and young adults. The world we live in is full of evil people who want to do horrible things. Take your precautions to try and prevent these things from happening and even then, sometimes they still do. I'll end with saying that if you want something, go and make it happen. I wanted to write for a long time but came up with many excuses. Everything from I didn't go to school to be a writer to what if people don't like it. In the end what counts is that you tried and that you are happy with the ending. Go out and do what you want to do. Life is short but opportunities is endless.

CHAPTER 1

DETECTIVE MARC CALDWELL sat at the coffee shop table staring at the Monday-morning newspaper. Across the top in bold letters was the headline *Briscoe Teen Reported Missing*. Caldwell took another drink of his coffee while he continued to scan the front page.

"So, I heard there's a girl who came up missing."

Detective Caldwell looked up to see the coffee shop barista looking expectantly in his direction. "Yes, unfortunately there is, what all have you heard?" he replied.

"Not a whole lot; people come in here day in and day out with all kinds of stories but I never know what to believe. Do you guys have any leads as to what might have happened to her, or is the whole thing still a complete mystery?"

Caldwell took another drink from his coffee and looked back down at the paper. "Well, right now, the whole damn thing is still a mystery."

The town of Briscoe, Texas, had a population of just under 50,000 people and up until now hadn't had many problems involving crime. Yes, being a junior college town, it had its fair share of college kid drama: DWIs, DUIs, complaints about loud music, and a few minor altercations. But there hadn't been a missing persons' report filed since August of 2015, when a thirteen-year-old girl had vanished. Four days later the police got a call from one of the local parents. Apparently, the teen had become upset with her parents and had been staying with a friend without responding to calls or text messages. The police apprehended her and returned her to her parents. It had now been over thirty hours and they weren't any closer to finding out what had happened to the now missing girl.

It was ten thirty that morning when Detective Caldwell returned to the station from questioning the missing girls' parents. He went to his office where there was a stack of files lying on his desk. As the senior detective on the police force, he had been assigned to the missing persons case. Walking over to his dry erase board, he picked up a black marker and scribbled on the surface of the board. He stepped back and observed the board: *Mercedes Vargas 16 YO last seen Saturday 10-01-2016.*

Walking back to his desk and sitting down, he grabbed the file with *Vargas, M* printed on the cover. He opened it to find photos of the victim along with her missing persons poster. The poster listed her as being five feet, four inches tall and weighing 120 pounds, last seen wearing a blue shirt, denim jeans, and brown boots. Looking at the photos, he felt a sense of sadness and anger building inside him. Mercedes had long, dark-brown hair with brown eyes and fair skin. In the photos she appeared happy, with a radiant smile. Around her neck was a silver-toned necklace with a cross hanging from it. He couldn't help but wonder if young Mercedes was still alive. Had she run away on her own or was she the victim of someone's evil plan? In his mind, he praised her parents for being as strong as they had been in his initial interview; he had no children of his own but couldn't imagine having a kid suddenly disappearing. From one hour to the next just gone, with no earthly idea what had happened. Now that must be torture.

When he'd spoken with Mercedes's parents at nine that morning, they described her as a smart, beautiful, funny girl with an amazing personality. "Everyone loved Mercedes; she had nothing but friends," Caldwell remembered her mother telling him. With Mercedes already being gone this long with no leads, he knew the odds of finding her alive were getting slim. The best time to solve a case or find clues that lead to the solving of a crime are in the first forty-eight hours after it is committed.

Detective Caldwell began to go over the time line notes that he had compiled outlining the past two days. Mercedes had met with three friends at the local movie theater around 9:45 p.m. on Saturday night. The movie finished around 11:30 p.m.; in his interviews, her friends stated that when the movie was over there weren't many cars left in the parking lot. The three friends left in the same vehicle they had ridden together in, and Mercedes had stayed behind expecting her mother to arrive soon. Mercedes's mother had stated that she had planned to pick Mercedes up around eleven thirty, but when she arrived in the parking lot it was empty. Assuming Mercedes had gotten a ride with her friends, she headed back home. "I thought, hey, maybe her phone is dead and that's why she didn't call me to tell me she had gotten a ride." Detective Caldwell remembered her saying with tear filled eyes and a trembling voice.

After arriving home around midnight, Mrs. Vargas called out for Mercedes but didn't get a response. Checking her room, she found that it was empty. "Her father was on the living room recliner watching television, so I asked him if Mercedes had come home. He said no." Mrs. Vargas immediately called one of the friends that had also been at the movies, who told her that Mercedes had stayed behind waiting for her to arrive. "I called her cell phone several times, but each time it went to voice mail. When she didn't arrive home by 2:00 a.m., that's when I called 911 to report her missing." Detective Caldwell remembered the words as if she had just said them, but he couldn't help but wonder why she had waited so long to call.

He knew that one of the main tactics for solving a crime is paying strict attention to detail. Request for the use of the local prison's scent-specific canines was submitted by Captain Cruz and granted. The dogs were at the movie theater parking lot by 3:00 a.m. and had tracked Mercedes's scent to the far corner of the lot and then back around to the entrance before exiting onto the highway. The Texas Department of Public Safety Highway Patrols assisted in shutting down one of the roads while the dogs continued to track the scent along the highway. The tracking continued until reaching the on ramp of the highway, and from there the scent went cold. Missing person posters were immediately printed and had already been posted at all of the local con-venience stores, and the story had made the Sunday morning newspaper headlines.

Being thirty-five hours into the case with few leads, Detective Caldwell decided to try another well-known tactic: hold an open press conference where Mercedes's parents would have their chance to address the case. It was a proven tactic that had worked well with similar cases. Something about the parents' genuine concern for the health and well-be-ing of their loved ones, combined with the amount of people a television broadcast could reach, had shown to be effective.

With the Briscoe Police Department never deal-ing with a kidnapping in the past, everything was moving slower than Detective Caldwell would have liked. Everything he was doing now he had either found in the missing persons manual or phoned oth-er agencies for advice.

On Tuesday morning at 9:00 a.m., Detective Caldwell was in touch with Mercedes's parents, ex-plaining this next move. They quickly agreed to par-ticipate in a press conference.

That night at 7:00 p.m., the conference was held in the local high school gymnasium. The turn-out from the community was huge, with hundreds of men, women, and children showing up. While

Detective Caldwell was coaching her parents on what to say, several of Mercedes classmates and friends spoke out to the media and to the community about her disappearance and how much they all wanted her home.

Finally, it was the Vargases turn to speak. Mrs. Vargas went first. She stepped up to the podium with tear filled eyes, wrinkled clothes, and messy hair. The audience could tell by the dark bags under her eyes that she hadn't slept much in the past few days. "First off, I want to thank Detective Caldwell for setting up this press conference and for Briscoe ISD for allowing us to use the gym. The constant effort he has put toward finding my baby can never be repaid."

She started to cry. "I miss my baby so much. You don't understand how hard it is for her not to be here. I cannot eat, I cannot sleep, I cannot do anything except wonder where you are and if you are OK. Baby, please, if you can hear this, and if it is something we have done, just come home. We will make it all right again."

Pausing for a moment to regain her composure she continued. "If you have taken my daughter, please, please bring her back home. She is my only child, my baby. I'll do anything, I'll pay anything, I'll give you anything, just please don't hurt my baby, just please bring her back to me." She began to sob again but this time so hard that she could no longer speak. Mercedes's father stepped up to comfort her as she faced into his chest, squeezing her arms around him and letting out a cry that could even be heard at the back of the gym.

By then everyone who had turned out for the conference was now in tears. Mercedes's father took his chance to speak. "Mija, I love you. Please come back home. If it is something we have done I promise you, baby . . . we can fix this. If you have taken my daughter, I beg you, please just bring my baby back. Whatever the cost, whatever you want, we just want our baby back. Te amo mucho, come home, mija." His attempts to hold back the tears dissolved, and he too began to cry uncontrollably. A group of local pastors and their wives stepped up to comfort them and helped them to the side of the gym where other officers were waiting.

Detective Caldwell approached the podium. "People of Briscoe and the surrounding communities, we need your help. Mercedes Vargas has gone missing. We have few leads, and we are relying on your assistance to help us find her. As you can see, she is missed dearly. I am sure those of you with children couldn't imagine being in this situation. Let us come together and bring one of Briscoe's very own back home to her family. If you have any information on the disappearance of Mercedes Vargas, please contact the Briscoe Police Department. Thank you."

CHAPTER 2

The sound of a door slamming shut woke her up from her sleep. The air in the room was freezing, and she wondered how she had even managed to sleep at all. The blindfold that had been tied around her eyes was still firmly in place, as well as tape around her mouth, wrist, and ankles. She could hear footsteps in the room and knew whoever had taken her was back. With each step, she waited in terror. The footsteps stopped. The room was silent. Then she heard him speak.

"I am going to remove the blindfold from your eyes and the tape from your mouth. We are miles from anything and no one will hear you if you try to scream; you'll only piss me off if you do."

The voice was muffled but she understood what he had said.

"If you cooperate with everything I say to do, then I will not harm you. But if you try to play me for a fool, then I won't hesitate to make your life a living hell . . . Do you understand?"

The footsteps circled around until they were positioned behind her. "I'm going to take the tape off now," he said. She felt the tug of the tape as he started peeling it away from her skin; it stung. Little by little he eased the tape back until it was fully removed. "Good," he said. "I'm going to take the blindfold off now, OK?"

"OK," Mercedes said in shaky voice. She felt the pressure of the blindfold tighten against her skin before it came off, revealing the room where she sat.

Even with the little light in the room, it took a few seconds for her eyes to adjust. Looking around, she tried to figure out where she was, but the room was a mystery. He wasn't standing directly behind her anymore, but she could still hear him. There must have been a desk or table where he was standing, and he was moving objects back and forth on its surface. She tried harder to turn around, but the restraints only allowed her to move so far.

"Why did you take me?" she said. "Why are you doing this?"

But there was no reply. He continued with the movement at the table, oblivious to what she was asking.

Mercedes began to plead with the man.

"Please, please let me go, I'll do any—" Before she could finish he cut her off midsentence.

"If you don't shut the hell up, I am going to start pulling your teeth out one by one, little girl. When I want you to talk, I'll ask you something. Is that clear?"

She closed her eyes and tried to remain calm. "Yes," she said.

As she sat in the chair unable to move her hands or feet, she felt herself beginning to get claustrophobic. He had said that if she screamed nobody would hear her, but what if he was just saying that just so she wouldn't scream? Here was her one chance. Who knew how long he would have the tape off her mouth? She had to give it a try.

"Help, help me!" she screamed as loud as she could. "Help!" She heard his footsteps and before she could let out another cry for help, he had circled around in front of her and she felt the full force of a punch to her stomach. All the air in her lungs was now gone.

"I am not playing with you, little bitch. This is your one warning."

She gasped, trying to breathe, but the air in the room was too cold to take in.

She felt his right hand take hold of her throat and begin to squeeze. The leather glove he was wearing created a slight cushioning effect, but he still managed to cut off her air supply. Mercedes could feel the pressure starting to build in the back of her eyes and in her ears. She had a brief moment to think to herself, *Is this it? Is this how it ends?* Then her vision went black.

The next time Mercedes opened her eyes, her immediate thought was *I'm not dead.* The next was about the pain she felt in her stomach from being punched. She lifted her head, trying to see where he had gone, and there he was: sitting in a chair directly across from her. It caught her by surprise.

He had on a mask, a scary one that resembled an evil scarecrow, and was wearing a black two-piece suit. It all made sense now why his voice had sounded muffled. He was also wearing black leather gloves and had one leg crossed over the other.

"Mercedes, you and I are going to play a little game. The name of the game is Let's Meet the Vargases. The night I took you, you told me that your mother was supposed to have picked you up at 11:30 p.m., right?"

Mercedes was quick to reply. "Yes, she said she was going to be out anyways, so she would stop by and get me before going home."

"You also told me that she has been spending a lot of time with a guy named Sam and that's where she was that night. Who is Sam?"

Mercedes started to cry.

"It's OK. You can tell me," he said.

"But I don't want to . . . I don't want to betray my mother like that."

"I am not asking you to betray anyone, Mercedes. I'm just asking you who Sam is."

"He's my mother's friend. They knew each other in high school, but he moved to another state, Georgia or something. Well, he moved back here to Texas about four months ago and one day Mom and I had gone out to get some things from the grocery store and she ended up running into him. They exchanged numbers, and he's been coming by to visit once or twice a week."

The man in the mask started to laugh. "Imagine that. Well, where is your dad at when Sam is making his weekly visits?"

"He's usually at work."

He continued to ask questions, and Mercedes continued to answer. At this point she knew better than to go against anything he said. He hadn't killed her last time, but it had been pretty close.

His questioning continued for what seemed like eternity. Finally he said, "OK, Mercedes, you have been a good girl. You've answered all the questions I've asked you. I'm going to give you this opportunity to ask me whatever you want, and I'll answer truthfully."

There was no doubt in her mind the number one question she wanted to ask. "Are you going to kill me?"

"Well, that depends," he said thoughtfully.

"Depends on what?"

"Depends on if you continue to cooperate."

His voice was quiet but firm, she knew he wasn't joking.

She leaned forward. "Why did you take me to begin with?"

"I took you to prove a point. People can't just be allowing their kids to do whatever they want and not expect consequences for those actions."

"But all I did was go to the movie with my friends."

"Yes . . . then sit in the dark by yourself till almost midnight. How old are you, sixteen? Your mother allowed her sixteen-year-old princess to stay stuck alone while she was out being a whore?"

"She is not a whore!" Mercedes screamed.

"Say what you want, but her actions say differently," he replied.

He stood up and walked toward Mercedes. Reaching out with his left hand, he ran it along the right side of her face.

"You are so cute; do you have a boyfriend?"

Mercedes quickly turned her head, causing his hand to fall from her face. He grabbed her hair with his left hand and pulled her head backward while grabbing her throat with his right.

"I asked you a fucking question," he said.

"No, my dad doesn't allow me to date yet. He always tells me to focus on my grades and that boys can wait."

With his grip on her throat she could barely finish her sentence, but fearing what he may do next gave her the strength to answer him.

"Wow, that makes you even more special to me. I know people who would buy you in a heartbeat."

He released her from his grip, and his hands fell to a resting position. "I got you some food. I am going to release you so that you can eat and use the restroom if you have to." He walked over to the table he had been at earlier and tried again to see him. It was no use; the restraints took away her full range of motion. She could hear the paper bag rustle as he grabbed it from the surface and returned quickly to where she was sitting. He reached in his pocket and pulled out a knife. Opening the blade, he knelt to one knee and slowly cut the tape that had been holding her ankles to the chair. Standing back up, he cut the tape that held her left wrist and then proceeded to cut the tape that held her right. "Remember what I said, Mercedes, no funny business."

She opened the bag and grabbed the hamburger from inside. "I have a question though," she said.

"Yes?"

"Where do I use the bathroom?"

Turning sideways he pointed to the back corner of the room. Looking in the direction he had pointed, she saw a single bucket positioned near the wall. Her immediate thought was that there was no wall or barrier separating the corner from the rest of the room, but she was too hungry to worry about the restroom area. She began to eat her burger, and in only a few bites it was gone. Fast food was quick and easy to grab, but the down side to that was the food usually wasn't much. But when she looked back in the bag, she saw there was another burger inside.

"Hurry up and finish," he said. "Then I am going to break it down real clear to you how this is going to work."

"How what is going to work?" she asked.

"Just finish," he said.

Mercedes took slower bites, trying to enjoy what was left of the burger. She tried not to think of what was going to happen and wondered how her mom and dad were. What were they doing, had they still been searching, or had they already given up? *Hold on, Mom*, she thought to herself. *I'll be home soon.*

CHAPTER 3

THE PRESS CONFERENCE had gone well, and the police were getting several reports daily. A couple passing through Silverton, Texas, on their way to Kansas reported they had seen Mercedes at a local convenient store. Detective Caldwell looked into the lead, but it turned out to be a local girl who bore a big resemblance to Mercedes. Another lead came from a truck driver who said he had seen her at a bus stop in Plainview, Texas. That tip eventually led to nothing as well. Then, a few days after the conference had been held, on Monday morning October 22, Caldwell received an anonymous letter in the mail.

The envelope was addressed to Detective Marc Caldwell but had no return address. There was one letter inside, folded into sections and sealed with a yellow smiley face sticker. As he began to read, he got that sick feeling in the pit of his stomach. He closed his eyes and folded the letter slowly; his hands had become sweaty. Then he opened the letter and once again began to read, this time all the way through.

Hey there, Detective, it's me—the one you and the town of Briscoe have been looking for! I got tired of you trying to find me without success, so I thought, hey, why not go to you! Your little press conference was so cute. I almost cried myself. Hahaha! That bitch put on one hell of a show up there. "OHHH, I want my baby back, I want my baby back." You know what I think is funny, Detective? Where was that whore when her baby was waiting for her at the movies? Sounds like somebody's time line is a little messed up! She allowed her teenage daughter to sit out there alone well past 11:45 p.m., so what did she think was going to happen? I was a wolf waiting for a snack. I didn't have to wait long, now did I? Do these people not watch or read the news? It absolutely amazes me that parents nowadays give their children so much freedom in a world where sex trafficking is a booming business. Yet society turns a blind eye to it while these people just disappear into the night like they were never there to begin with.

Sooo, Detective, how much do you think I can get for this one, a young teenager with long brown hair and brown eyes? I'm sure one of these perverts is willing to take her off my hands. Word of advice, unless you want me ending up with another one of your Briscoe teens, I suggest you put the word out for parents to watch their kids more carefully. Oh, and in case you don't think I have pretty little Mercedes, you'd better take another look into that envelope! Have a NICE day!

P.S. The sand is flowing . . .

Detective Caldwell immediately reached for the envelope. Looking inside he found a photo of Mercedes. She was sitting upright in a metal chair, wearing the clothes she was last seen in. All four of her limbs were bound to the chair with duct tape, and she was blindfolded. The room was dark with just enough light for a clear picture to be taken.

He flashed back to the conversations he had been having with Mercedes parents, they called everyday checking for updates in the case and he would now be able to give them one. He was lost in thought wondering if she had been harmed and if so how bad, when the ringing of his office phone caught him off guard, causing him to flinch. "This is Detective Caldwell speaking."

"Yes, this is Sharon Woods from the local newspaper. We have something we think you need to look at."

He leaned forward, putting his elbows on to his desk. "What is it that you have, what does it have to do with?"

"I would rather just show you in person, is there any way I can just meet you at the station?" she asked.

"Yes, that's fine. I'll let the front desk know to send you up to the office."

"OK then, I'll be there shortly." She said.

Hanging up the phone, he thought to himself, *What could it be?*

While waiting for Sharon to arrive, he picked up the phone and got in contact with Mrs. Vargas.

"Yes, Mrs. Vargas, it's Detective Caldwell. Listen, I am going to need you to come down to the station. I have a few more questions I want to ask you about the night Mercedes disappeared."

There was a pause on the other end of the phone line before she answered back.

"What, but Detective, I have already told you about that night several times. Have you heard anything else about my baby?"

Her response and the sound of her voice caught Detective Caldwell off guard, he wondered to himself if she was hiding something.

"Yes, I know, but I need to ask you a few more. Just come down to the office as soon as you can. No big hurry."

"OK, Detective Caldwell, whatever helps bring my baby home."

He rang off and made another call.

"Hello, Detective Shawn Peterson."

"Yo, Shawn, it's Marc. I want to ask if you could do me a favor. Can you head out to the address of Mr. and Mrs. Vargas?"

"The missing girl's parents? Sure, what's going on?"

"Well, I just think there may be something Mrs. Vargas isn't being honest about. Can you run surveillance on her for me?"

"I got you, bro. I'll head that direction now," Peterson said.

"I appreciate it. I owe you one," Caldwell said before hanging up the phone.

He remembered the day that Shawn had been promoted to Detective a year and a half ago. Fairly young, he was eager from the start to help out where he could. Detective Caldwell had taken him under his wing and was happy to be his mentor, now the two would be working on the most important case of their careers.

He picked up the new photo of Mercedes and began to scan it for clues. He could see that the young girl had been crying. A stream of tears leftover from her mascara was visible even in the low light of the room.

The picture brought back memories from his broken childhood. Like Mercedes, his sister too had been abducted when she was only thirteen. His family had received pictures similar to the ones he was now holding, only his sister was never found. This had been the very reason he was now serving in law enforcement.

He heard someone walking down the hallway in the direction of his office, and then there was a knock at the door. "Come in," he said. The door opened slowly; it was Sharon from the newspaper.

"Please, please, come in. Grab a seat. Now what was it you were needing to tell me?" he asked.

"It's about the missing girl. Today I received a letter that has to be from whoever it was that had taken Mercedes. Here, this was in the envelope also." She said eagerly while reaching across the table, placing a picture onto the desk in front of Detective Caldwell. *It's the same picture*, he thought to himself.

"Where is the letter?" he asked.

Reaching into her computer bag, she pulled out the letter. Like the one he had received, Sharon's envelope had no return address either. Detective Caldwell pulled out the letter and quickly scanned over it. *I almost cried myself . . . Where was that whore when her baby was waiting for her at the movies? . . . I suggest you put the word out for parents to watch their kids more carefully.* The letter was the same as the one he had received.

Caldwell sat back in his chair with a sigh. "I'm going to keep this letter and its contents. I'll be sending it to the state lab in Austin to see if they can get any positive fingerprints."

"OK," Sharon replied, "but what about his request to inform the parents about their kids? I don't want to see any others come up missing."

Caldwell shook his head. "I don't either. I will be meeting with the chief of police and the Mayor later today. Together we will come up with a new plan of action. I am thinking of having the Mayor set a city-wide curfew, but I'll definitely keep you guys at the news station up to date on any information we get together."

She smiled and reached across the table, shaking Detective Caldwell's hand.

"I'll be looking forward to hearing from you," she said before standing up. Caldwell also stood up from his chair and walked her to the door.

"Together we will get this thing figured out." He opened the door, and she headed back in the direction of the front office.

Walking to his desk, he sat down. Leaning back, he tried to determine what the next option was. Mrs. Vargas had not arrived. Reaching over to the minifridge that sat by his desk, he opened the door, grabbed an energy drink from the top rack, and opened it. Taking a long drink, he shut the door to the fridge and again faced his desk. "I am going to find you, you snake, wait and see," he said quietly to himself.

Judging by the pictures, he knew Mercedes was still alive. Now it was just a matter of who was smarter at this cat-and-mouse game. He looked over at the clock: 2:00 p.m. He picked up the phone and dialed the number written on the sticky note stuck to the bottom right corner of his desk before placing the receiver to his ear. It rang twice before there was an answer on the other end.

"Mayor's office, how may we direct your call?"

"Yes, ma'am, this is Detective Caldwell. Can you get me the Mayor please?"

"Can you hold for one moment?" The line wasn't silent long. "Detective, the Mayor wishes to hear from you. I'll patch you through."

CHAPTER 4

I T WAS MONDAY, October 10, and back at the police station Detective Caldwell was preparing to interview Mrs. Vargas again. She had finally shown up at the station, and he was still looking for any missing pieces that would help with the investigation.

They walked back to interview room number three which was located in a section of the station separate from everything else. The room was cold and windowless and the only thing on the walls was a clock. They sat down across from Detective Caldwell and he started the interview.

"Mrs. Vargas, the night you were supposed to pick up Mercedes from the movie theater, where were you?"

"I had gone to Walmart to pick up a few things I was needing for the house, and from there I went to the theater. By the time I got there Mercedes was no longer there."

Caldwell said, "I have spoken with the cashiers who were working at Walmart that night to see if they saw anyone suspicious in the store the night of the disappearance. They did not mention seeing you there."

Mrs. Vargas looked down at her hands. She had begun to fidget with her fingers. Mr. Vargas, who was also present, looked at her and then back to Detective Caldwell. Mrs. Vargas had asked Mr. Vargas several times not to come to the station but he insisted on being there arguing that Mercedes was his daughter too.

"Are you sure you spoke to everyone there?" he said. "I mean, I know she wasn't home. She had left and said that is where she was going."

Detective Caldwell replied, "I'm sure. I have spoken with everyone who was there that night, the Walmart being that close to the movie theater, and I also looked at the surveillance footage from the parking lot. I didn't see her car enter or leave the parking lot in that two-hour time frame."

Mrs. Vargas, who had still been looking at her hands, turned and faced Mr. Vargas. "¿Que pasa, Laura?" he said with a concerned look on his face. She began to cry and turned her head down toward her hands again.

Mr. Vargas was immediately upset. He quickly stood up from the chair where he had been sitting and asked her again, "What is going on? If you weren't at the store, then where were you for the two hours you were gone from the house?"

She was crying so hard she couldn't answer him. Detective Caldwell again asked her where she had been. "I can't do this right now!" she screamed back. "It's too much. I just need to breathe right now." Caldwell stood and opened the interview room door allowing, Mrs. Vargas to step out into the hallway.

Mr. Vargas immediately demanded, "What do mean you didn't see her vehicle in the parking lot? If she wasn't there, then where was she?"

Caldwell shook his head and spoke calmly. "I don't know, Mr. Vargas. All I know is she wasn't there. I am trying to get as many details together as I can. Maybe something will lead to a break in the case."

Mr. Vargas stepped out into the hallway, closing the interview room door behind him. Detective Caldwell could barely hear the conversation taking place, but clearly it wasn't good.

"You need to quit lying to the cop and tell him the truth," Mr. Vargas said angrily. "Do it for Mercedes."

"There is something that I need to tell you." Mrs. Vargas's voice was shaking. "I have been seeing somebody else."

"You have been what? What the hell are you talking about?"

"That night I was with somebody else, an old friend I know from high school."

The conversation had gone from a low-tone casual talk to a full-blown argument. Detective Caldwell opened the door.

"What's going on?" he said.

Mr. Vargas replied, "Apparently she has been talking to someone else despite us being married fifteen years. Do me a favor and find my daughter." He immediately stormed off.

Mrs. Vargas was leaned over with her head in her hands, and she had again begun to cry.

"Mrs. Vargas, what is going on?"

"I've been cheating on him with another man, an old friend I knew in high school."

This was news Detective Caldwell did not want the public to get wind of. With Mercedes gone, the public needed to see a unified front between Mr. and Mrs. Vargas. What would they think if they knew Mercedes being taken could have been as a result of Mrs. Vargas being unfaithful in her marriage.

Gently he guided Mrs. Vargas back into the interview room and got the rest of the story from her. The night she was with her friend Sam, she had lost track of time and had arrived late to pick up Mercedes.

Caldwell thought of the letter from the abductor and how it mentioned Mrs. Vargas not being on time. Whoever had abducted Mercedes had either known about her mother's affair or Mercedes had told them about it. Had this been part of their plan, to find out any negative information about the Vargas's and humiliate them on a public level?

Caldwell walked back to his office, where he still had Mercedes's file open on his desk. He closed the folder and pushed it to the corner of the desk. He reached for a laptop computer that lay closed on the opposite corner of the desk and grabbed it. Pulling it to the center of the desk he opened it and logged in.

He started a search for Sam Gonzales, the man who Mercedes mother had been having the affair with. His background was clean. Besides the search, Sam had been with Mrs. Vargas the night of the abduction eliminating him as the one who took her.

His next plan was to open a search for all the sex offenders living in the area. Whoever had taken Mercedes just might be on that list. Opening the search, he quickly realized narrowing the options would be no easy task. In Briscoe alone, there was twenty-six registered sex offenders and a total of fifty-four if the search was extended to the surrounding three towns.

Throughout the day he managed to shrink the list to ten possible assailants. It was outdated, and some of the offenders had moved to another town while others were back in prison serving time for other offenses.

With the list narrowed, Caldwell decided to call it a day and headed home. He hadn't had much sleep the past few days, he was working overtime on the case and was now running on fumes. Despite almost dozing off a few times on the way home, he finally made it.

After grabbing a quick bite to eat and showering, he lay down in bed. There had been many times in his career when he'd had to stay up for long periods of time, and each time he finally got to lie down, the comfort of his own bed was heaven. He wasn't lying there long when he finally dozed off.

***

"Get back here!" he screamed, running full speed behind a man in a black hoodie. The chase continued to an abandoned building and up the fire exit staircase. Floor by floor they made their way to the top of the ten-story building.

After making it to the top, he realized the assailant was nowhere in sight. Detective Caldwell reached to his side and pulled out the standard issued .40-caliber pistol and pointed it in front of him. The rooftop was dark with very little light to help him see. He tried feeling around the pockets of his work jacket looking for the flashlight he usually kept. He thought to himself, *Damnit, I must have left it at home. When I need it I don't have it on me.* Bringing his hand back up to stabilize the gun, he slowly walked forward, searching the area for the man in the hoodie.

Scanning left to right and right to left, he walked along the edge of the building. A loud bang startled him, and he quickly turned in the direction it had come from. A trash can lid was still bobbing side to side while lying upside down on the rooftop.

He turned and slowly made his way toward the lid, being more cautious as he got closer. "Why don't you just quit your shit and come out and talk to me!" he screamed out. He made it to the lid and continued walking, scanning the area for the man.

Another crash echoed from the opposite corner of the rooftop. He turned again, scanning the area in the direction the crash had come from. "Looking for me?" he heard someone say, but by the time his eyes were back in the right direction he felt the full force of someone pushing him.

He was so close to the edge of the building that it didn't take much effort for the hooded man to push him off. Detective Caldwell was now falling full speed from the ten-story building with his mind moving too fast to even think. There wasn't enough time for him to even scream, and just as he was about to hit the ground he jumped from his sleep to the sound of his phone ringing.

Still breathing hard, he reached for his phone and answered the call.

"Hey, Marc, it's Shawn. You might want to get down to the station; there's been another one."

"Another what?" Detective Caldwell asked.

"Another abduction."

CHAPTER 5

SHE HEARD THE door open, waking her from her sleep. Before leaving Scarecrow had secured her hands and feet back to the chair with duct tape and had also put the blindfold back over her eyes so that she could once again only see total darkness.

Hearing the noises that followed, Mercedes knew that he had another girl. There was the faint sounds of screams muffled with tape.

She heard the kidnapper say, "OK now, just go with the flow and I won't hurt you." Things seemed to be going the way he wanted until she heard him scream, "You stupid little bitch, you just had to do something stupid, right? Well, now I am going to show you."

Mercedes heard him walk toward the counter behind her and start shifting the objects there. After a few moments, she heard him walking back in the direction he had come from. Then it happened, the sound made her jump in her seat. Loud pops echoed in sequence followed by a loud buzzing sound. Then she heard the muffled scream again, only it continued. Finally, the sound stopped, but she could hear the sobs coming from whoever it was sitting across from her.

"Now why did you make me do this?" he said. "It could have gone a lot smoother, but you wanted to make it harder on yourself, didn't you?"

There was no reply, and Mercedes knew why. She heard him walking in her direction, where he removed the blindfold. At first everything was a blur and it took a few seconds for her sight to come back clear. There seated across from her was another girl.

"Are you needing to use the restroom yet?" he asked.

Mercedes replied, "No." It had only been around an hour since he had left.

"Well, you see I brought you some company. I didn't want you getting lonely down here." He laughed. "Don't mind her; she wanted to act up, so I had to give the ol' girl some act-right."

He held out the cattle prong taser, and it began to pop. She could see the bright spark of electric current as it jumped back and forth at the tip. "I got a new toy. What you think?" he asked as he laughed to himself. Then his voice rose. "I am going to tell you right now that as long as you both do what I ask, you won't be hurt! Do I make myself clear?" he screamed. "I'm talking to your little ass, too! I bet you won't kick me again."

He looked back at the girl in the opposite chair then back toward Mercedes. Stepping back from her chair, he walked back to the table where he sat the cattle prong back down.

He walked back to the chair where the other girl was sitting and removed the blindfold from her head and the tape from her mouth. Mercedes could see the girl had light brown hair with red and blond highlights. Her face was red, and her eyes were still watery from where she had been crying. She didn't look to be older than about sixteen, but Mercedes had never seen her before.

It took a moment for the girl's eyes to adjust, but when they did she quickly closed them and moved her head in a downward motion so that she could no longer see the evil staring back at her. It gave Mercedes flashbacks to the time she'd first seen him; the mask alone could give somebody nightmares.

The girl slowly lifted her head until she was looking forward again; she noticed Mercedes sitting across from her and gasped. "You're that girl from the press conference . . . Mercedes Vargas. Oh my God, you're still alive! That's good, that's really good," she said while trying not to cry.

Mercedes had nothing to say. She sat there quietly just staring back at the other girl as if she were frozen in time. The kidnapper began to ask the new girl questions first starting with her name.

"What's your name?"

"Michelle . . . Michelle Foster," she said in a shaky voice.

"OK, Michelle, I'm going to tell you like I told Mercedes over there, as long as you're cooperating with me, I promise I won't hurt you, deal?"

"OK . . . OK, sure," she said.

"I'm going to set some ground rules. Once again we are in the middle of nowhere and nobody can hear you. If you scream you will only piss me off, and then I will have to hurt you like I did earlier. Do you understand?"

"Yes, I understand," she replied hastily, clearly not wanting to be shocked again. She hesitated, then added, "Can I ask you a question? Why did you choose to take me? Why did you choose to take her?"

"First off, I ask the questions here. Second, I took you because it was too easy. I had already taken her, so I figured the rest of the town would know better than to allow their kids to be out after dark. Let me guess, is your mother a whore like hers?"

He turned quickly, pointing in the direction of Mercedes. But before he could turn back around Mercedes out of anger uttered, "Fuck you," under her breath. He began to laugh out loud.

"Oh, is that right, fuck me? Is that what you want, you want to fuck me?" he asked.

He had now turned and was fully facing Mercedes. He walked slowly to the chair where she sat and reached out with his left hand, grabbing the right side of her face.

Leaning in he asked again, "You want to fuck me, Mercedes?"

She spat at him, hitting the mask he was wearing directly front and center. Quickly pulling his arm back, he released the full force of a punch, hitting Mercedes right in the mouth. She didn't scream but made an awkward noise, he had the breath knocked out of her. He drew back and punched her two more times in the mouth.

The blows had knocked Mercedes unconscious. Quickly the kidnapper began to tear the tape holding her arms and legs to the chair. Her body was motionless, and he struggled with the dead weight, but he managed to pick her up and leaned her face down over the arms of the chair.

Turning to look at Michelle, he yelled, "You better not say a fucking word! Any little sound out of you and you are getting the shock treatment again."

As much as she wanted to scream, as much as she wanted to help, Michelle knew that she couldn't. She couldn't move, and screaming would do no good; it would only aggravate him enough to want to hurt her too.

Once the kidnapper had taped Mercedes's arms back to the arm of the chair closest to her torso, he quickly moved around behind her. Using the tape, he began to secure her legs to the chair by running the tape around her thighs just above the knee and back around to the arm of the chair positioned under her hips. Finishing the tape, he went to the table and returned with a new roll. Using more tape, he continued to wrap her legs until they were held firmly in place.

Michelle was still watching, and she knew it wasn't good. Mercedes was breathing but she had blood dripping from out of her mouth now. Based on the position she was in and the amount of tape he'd used, she knew Mercedes wasn't going anywhere.

She could tug and wiggle all day long in an attempt to get free, but even that wouldn't work.

"Now then, let's just wait for her to wake up. I wouldn't want her to miss what's fixing to happen."

Grabbing the tape, he went back to where Mercedes's head lay. Using the roll, he went twice around her head and mouth before tearing the tape. Turning toward the table, he tossed the roll and it landed on the surface with a thud.

He walked over to where Michelle was sitting and stood there. Reaching down with his right hand, he began to run it through her hair. Michelle closed her eyes, trying not to think about what was going on. "You sure are pretty, you know that? I would hate for something bad to happen to you. Then you wouldn't be worth as much money."

Five minutes went by, and Mercedes slowly started to move her head. She didn't realize at first that she had been taped in the awkward position, but when she did she started to move her head from side to side, looking around.

"Well, look who finally woke up and decided to join the party—well, my party at least."

The kidnapper walked back over to where Mercedes was tied and stood behind her. "So, fuck me, huh?" he said as he reached down and started groping her buttocks. Her eyes widened, and she looked to Michelle for help, but there was no use; Michelle was frozen. She tried and tried to move, but she was helpless.

Reaching around Mercedes's waist, he unbuttoned her pants and began to peel them back. Mercedes tried frantically to move, but even with all her effort she didn't budge. Her eyes grew wide with fear.

Pulling her pants back took little effort for him. *Who is this monster?* she thought to herself. Closing her eyes, she only had one thought left: *God, please help me.*

The thought was an unanswered prayer. He pulled his jeans down and forced himself inside her. "You like that?" he asked while taking hold of her hair.

Mercedes jerked her head back in pain as the rape started. She tried to turn and look at Michelle for help, but Michelle was stuck there as if frozen in time. Tied to the chair, she was helpless. Michelle finally closed her eyes and tilted her head down in shame, wishing she didn't have to hear the sound of what was going on a few feet away.

Mercedes tried to scream, but with the tape around her mouth it was useless. Tears began to fall from her eyes as the monster continued his evil act.

He pulled her hair and squeezed the back of her neck as the rape continued for another three minutes; by the time it was over Mercedes's head hung down. She was motionless, her spirit broken, and she thought to herself, *God, just take me. I don't want to be alive anymore.*

CHAPTER 6

IT DIDN'T TAKE Detective Caldwell long to get back to the police station. When he arrived, Peterson already had another missing persons file ready.

"When did it happen?" Caldwell asked.

"She was reported missing about three hours ago. She went to a home coming decoration event with her friends and from there she was supposed to walk home. When she didn't make it home, her parents got worried and started to call around. When they weren't able to locate her, they called us."

"Why in the hell do these parents keep doing this? Do they not understand it isn't safe for their children to be out right now?" He said in an angry voice.

"Well, the thing is, her house is only a block away from the football field," Detective Peterson said.

He handed the file to Caldwell, who opened it. Inside was another picture of a teenage girl: *Michelle Foster, 5'7" 128 lbs., last seen leaving Briscoe High School basketball gym.* There was also a picture her wearing a light blue polo-style shirt with dark blue jeans. She had light skin with dark brown hair and a big smile that lit up the photo.

"So, do we have any leads?" Caldwell asked with a sigh. He felt sick to his stomach.

"Well, nothing yet, sir. Family and friends have been out doing a search of the area, but it's turned up nothing."

"What was she last seen wearing?"

"Her mother said that she was wearing blue jeans and a red hoodie with the school's logo on it."

"Have you contacted the prison to ask if we can use their scent canines?"

"Yes sir, they are already on the scene. Even the unit warden showed up to assist in any way he could."

Caldwell walked around his desk and to the dry erase board, where he had already written Mercedes's name. Grabbing the blue marker, he took off the lid and wrote *Michelle Foster 16 YO last seen 10-07-16.* Stepping back, he looked at the two names that were now on the board and thought to himself, *I'm going to find you both. Just hang on.*

"Are you OK, bro?" Peterson asked.

"I'm good, I'm good, just want so badly to bring these girls back to their parents, you know."

"Yeah, I know what you mean. You know you got this, we believe in you, and Captain Cruz . . . he believes in you, too, or he wouldn't have given you the cases. I'm going to go grab some coffee for us. Anything else you need?"

"How about a beer?" Detective Caldwell said jokingly.

"Oh, come on now, you know you don't need that stuff." Peterson gave a brief laugh. "I'll be back in a little bit."

He left, closing the door behind him. Caldwell walked over to the TV and turned it on. It was still on the news. He went back to his office chair and sat down. Connecting his cell phone to the charger, he laid it on the desk. The local news channel still displayed *Missing Teen* flashing across the bottom of the screen.

His cell phone buzzed, and he reached down to pick it up; it was the amber alert for Michelle Foster. *16 YO Michelle Foster 5'7" brown hair brown eyes last seen leaving Briscoe football game.*

The alert troubled him, but at least he knew that everyone was assisting in finding the two girls. He turned his attention back to the TV, where the news anchor was urging parents to keep their children inside after dark or accompany them wherever they were going. The top left corner displayed a small map that flashed *Winter Storm Warning* in red letters, and he thought to himself, *Damn, all we need is snow to add more to this mess.*

His desk phone started ringing, causing him to jump. He smiled to himself, thinking, *I'm a damn chicken*, before reaching over to pick it up.

"Hello, Detective Marc Caldwell speaking."

The voice on the other end of the line was male and sounded distraught. "Yes, Detective, I'm calling because I think I may have a lead on the two girls who are missing."

Caldwell was wide awake now. Reaching quickly for a pen and a piece of paper, he continued the conversation. "OK great, what kind of lead do you have?"

There was a pause. "I think I know who may have taken them."

Caldwell's heart began to race. "Who, who do you think took them?"

There was another pause. "I think I took them, you idiot." The man on the other end of the phone line started laughing.

Caldwell was instantly furious, he slammed one hand on the table and felt blood begin to rush to his face. "Listen here, you sick son of a bitch, you think this is funny? There are worried families waiting for those girls to come home, and you want to be playing?"

"Did I say I was playing, Detective?' His voice was now serious. "Before you start running your mouth on the other end of this damn phone, I think you better know who you are talking to. I have your little angels sitting right here."

"Why are you doing this?" Detective Caldwell asked.

"I know you got the letter I wrote. I told you in that letter why I did what I am doing, and it's only going to continue unless these parents start using their brains."

Caldwell was frantic. "Have you hurt them? Are they still alive?"

"Oh, they're still alive. They may have a few bumps and bruises here and there"—he barked a short laugh—"but nothing a little time can't take care of."

"What do you want? What do we have to do to get the girls back?"

"You let me think about that for a little while, and I'll get back to you. Well, Detective, I guess I should be going. Now don't forget, the sand is flowing . . ."

The man started laughing again before the phone line clicked, sending out the busy signal.

"Damn it!" Caldwell screamed, slamming the phone on the receiver. Picking it back up, he slammed it twice more.

The office door flew open. "What in the hell are you doing in here?" It was Detective Peterson; he had a drink carrier with two cups inside of it.

"You're never going to believe this," Caldwell said.

Peterson took one of the cups and handed it to him. "What happened?"

"That son of a bitch just called me. He has both girls."

"Wait, what?"

"Yeah, he just called me on my office phone."

"Well, what did he say?"

"At first he pretended to be someone who was going to provide a tip, so I got ready to take down the information. Then he said he was the one who had taken them, that he had the girls right there with him."

Peterson began to laugh to himself. "Man, he is brave, isn't he?"

Caldwell took a drink of his coffee then picked up the phone and dialed zero. "Nancy, can you let the guys in the IT department know that they need to put a bug on my office phone sometime tomorrow? . . . OK, thank you."

"Oh, you're going old school on him," Peterson said.

Tapping a phone line had been a go to method of tracing phone calls in the past and one that hadn't been used often in Briscoe.

"I'll do whatever I have to do to catch that piece of shit."

The IT department was in Caldwell's' office first thing the next morning. He had slept on the love seat sofa, not wanting to leave his office and risk missing a call from the kidnapper if he decided to call back.

"OK, Detective, the monitor is tied in. You should be set up and ready to go. If you get another call, just contact one of us and we can come up here and let you know where the call was placed from."

With Briscoe being a smaller community, its technology was still out dated with even the office phones being rotary dial. Each year a request for better equipment was submitted, but each year it was shot down. It was always argued that if there wasn't any violence in the small town, then why waste the money.

"Thanks, Logan, Gabe, I sure appreciate it," Caldwell said as the two left.

He went back to his desk with the files for the two missing girls. Logging into his computer, he checked the local towns and cities to see if there had been any missing girls reported in other areas close to Briscoe, but there weren't.

He picked up his phone and dialed Peterson.

"It's Marc. Do you have any new leads on the Foster case?"

Being wrapped up in the Vargas case, he had assigned Peterson to deal with any of the leads or new information dealing with the Michelle Foster case on the night she had been taken. He could rely on him to do the groundwork but ultimately the case was assigned to him and the responsibility to find the girls laid on him.

"Well, I'm just here at the parents' house. They don't have any new information. I've been speaking with some of her friends that are here, just seeing if they knew of anyone who might want to hurt her, but nothing has come up."

"All righty, sounds good. I'll let you get back to that; just let me know if you get anything new."

Setting his phone back down, Caldwell closed his eyes and leaned back in the chair, crossing his arms behind his head. He thought to himself, *I'm tired, I'm sleepy, give me the strength to keep moving.*

He felt himself slowly drifting to sleep; his eyelids felt heavy and his body was relaxed. He was barely going into a dream state when his office phone rang, causing him to pop forward in the chair.

He reached for the phone, juggling the receiver as he brought it to his head.

"Hello, Detective Caldwell speaking."

"Why hey there, Detective. I see you have some new software on that phone of yours."

He recognized the voice and it instantly upset him.

"What the hell are you talking about?"

"A little birdy told me you've placed a tracker on your office phone. That's not fair. You're going to use computers to help you try and catch me?"

"I don't give a damn about catching you. I just want those girls back at home safe."

"Try selling your lies to somebody else. Isn't that your job, Detective? Isn't it your job to try and catch the bad guy?"

"You're not a bad guy; you're a coward hiding in the shadows."

"A coward?" The man laughed loudly, as if highly amused. "Of course you would say that. Whatever you can do to make me mad and cause me to slip up. Well, I'll tell you what, Detective, the ball is in my court and the only way you'll get these girls back or catch me is if I allow you to. You are good at what you do, but I don't think you've ever met a guy like me."

Detective Caldwell knew that with the departments outdated technology he needed to keep whoever was on the other end of the phone talking in order for the software to detect where the call was placed from. But how had he known that the software was on the phone to begin with? His mind drifted for a second and he thought to himself, *Somebody here has to be telling this guy stuff. There is no way he should know this.* He zoned back into the conversation.

"Look, this isn't about you right now. As long as those girls are found safe then you can leave and nobody will ever know anything."

"Well, Detective, I'm not quite so sure it works that way, but I'll keep your offer on the line." He laughed again. His laugh was really beginning to piss Caldwell off. "Well, I got to get going now. P. S., the sand is flowing."

The phone went to the sound of a busy signal, and Detective Caldwell immediately hung up. Picking it back up, he called the guys from IT.

"IT department, this is Logan."

"Hey, Logan, it's Detective Caldwell. I need you to get up here and check this machine. The kidnapper just called."

"Ok, awesome, we'll be right there."

Caldwell hung up the phone, but his mind went right back to how the kidnapper could have known that there was a bug on it to begin with.

It took Gabe and Logan a little over five minutes to get to his office. Their department was located on the second floor while the detective offices were located on the sixth. As soon as they arrived, they went straight to the monitor, where they began typing information into the side computer that was connected to the phone.

"You have anything yet?" Caldwell asked eagerly.

"We're running the scan right now; it should take less than three minutes."

Time seemed to stand still during the wait. When Caldwell looked back at the clock, it had been almost five minutes already.

"Is there something wrong? It's already been five minutes."

"Sorry, sir, it doesn't normally take this long, we are just . . ." Before Logan could finish his sentence, the computer started to make a beeping noise, cutting him off.

"Wow, you're not going to believe this, Detective. That phone call was placed from somewhere inside this building."

"What? What do you mean, in this building?"

Logan looked at him with wide eyes. "Whoever placed that last call to you used one of the phones from inside our building."

55

CHAPTER 7

ERCEDES WOKE UP still slumped over the chair where he had left her after she had cried herself to sleep. Raising her head to look around, she saw that Michelle had fallen asleep also. The air in the room was cold on her skin; he had left her there naked from the waist down. For someone to do what he had done . . . she knew the man she was dealing with wasn't your normal day-to-day person. He had to be sick in the head.

She heard movement from the direction of the entry sliding metal door, and it finally flew open. There he was, wearing the same scarecrow mask that he had been wearing since the day he'd taken her. He was carrying two grocery sacks and took them to the table, where he sat them down.

"Wake up," he said as he approached Michelle.

Waking up and seeing him with the mask on, she immediately closed her eyes and turned her head downward.

"Pick your head up; it's just me," he said. "I'm going to untie you so you can help Mercedes, OK? You better not try anything funny or I promise to make your life a living hell."

He reached into his pocket and pulled out a knife. Unfolding the blade, he cut through the tape until all her limbs were free. He stepped back, and she got up from the chair. Walking hesitantly toward Mercedes, she looked back at him for approval.

"Go on now, that's the reason I cut you free," he said.

When she reached Mercedes, her first thought was to help get her pants back on. Reaching down to take hold, she immediately pulled her hands back. The pants were wet and smelled of urine. Sometime during the past couple of hours she had peed on herself and hadn't even realized it.

"Her pants are wet," she said as she turned to look at him.

"And what the hell do you want me to do about it?" he replied.

Michelle knew it wasn't worth asking him to get Mercedes a change of clothes; that had to be the last thing on his mind. She reached again for the pants and pulled them up to Mercedes waist. She knew it wouldn't be the most comfortable feeling right now, but at least Mercedes would be covered. Mercedes had begun to shake from how cold the temperature was in the room, and Michelle worked as quickly as she could to get her untied.

When Mercedes was free, Michelle helped her to a standing position. She moved slowly, taking tiny steps as if she was barely learning how to walk. She squinted her eyes and started to cry; lifting her hands to cover her face, she buried her head in them. Michelle gave her a hug, attempting to comfort her.

The man in the mask turned and walked toward the table where he had set down the grocery bags. Reaching inside the first bag, he pulled out a pack of toilet paper, a few bottles of water, and a pack of wet wipes. Setting the items on the table, he reached into the other bag and pulled out a package of plastic forks, disposable bowls, a few cans of ravioli, and a few cans of soup. He turned and looked at the girls, who were still huddled next to each other.

"I got you girls food and some other things. Mercedes, I'll get you a change of clothes next time I'm in town."

Michelle walked quickly to the table and grabbed the packet of wet wipes. Walking back over to Mercedes, she tore open the pack and pulled out a few. She handed them to Mercedes, who used them to wipe her face.

"I'm going to be heading back into town," the kidnapper said. "I'll also get you guys a couple of blankets. It's getting cold out and they are expecting a snowstorm."

Michelle, who had her attention on him now, turned back toward Mercedes.

"Do you want me to get you some soup?"

Mercedes answered, "Ye-ye-yes," trying to get the words out while shaking from the cold.

The kidnapper walked toward the entrance door and without saying a word slid it open and then back closed behind him. They could hear the sound of metal tapping against metal and knew he was securing the door with a chain or a padlock, or maybe both. It was quiet for a few seconds, and they heard the sound of another door sliding open and then closed.

Wherever he had them, it was certainly a place he knew would be hard for anyone to escape from or for anyone to hear any screams that might be coming from within.

"That asshole raped me; he really raped me," Mercedes said.

"I'm so sorry, Mercedes. You don't know how hard it was to be stuck there watching knowing that

I couldn't help you. But at least you are alive; we still have hope."

"You still have hope," Mercedes said. "He took something from me that I will never get ba—"

"But you're alive," Michelle said cutting her off midsentence. "We still have hope, we are going to make it through this together. Look, I know it didn't happen to me. But I promise, life isn't over. You have tons of people who love you and want you home, we are going to make it through this."

"My pants are wet," Mercedes said, tilting her head down. "I peed all over myself."

"He said he would get you some clothes. Do you want to use my hoodie to wrap around you? At least it will be something dry."

"I'll try it," Mercedes said, still shaking.

Michelle removed her hoodie and handed it to Mercedes, who took it and began to walk to the corner of the room. "Wait, take a few of these," Michelle said, handing her the wet wipes. Once in the corner, Mercedes unbuttoned her pants and slid them off. She then used the wipes to get the areas her wet pants had been touching. Taking the unzipped neck area of the hoodie, she stretched the fabric and formed it around her waist. Reaching for the zipper she closed the front, making a makeshift skirt. She then pulled the hoodie's arms together and tied them in a knot.

Mercedes turned around and walked back to where Michelle was standing. While she had been changing, Michelle had gone to the table where she had opened two cans of soup and had already poured them from the can into the disposable bowls. Turning around, she handed one of the bowls to Mercedes and reached back to grab them both forks. The two went back to their chairs, where they sat down and ate in silence.

When they were finished eating, Michelle grabbed two bottles of water, handing one of them to Mercedes.

"So, what do you think he's going to do with us?" Michelle asked.

"I don't know. I had been hopeful he wouldn't hurt us. I should have just kept my mouth shut."

"How is your mouth feeling?" Michelle asked.

Mercedes reach up, patting her mouth with her right hand. She gave a soft moan. "It's really sore," she said.

"Look at me; let me see."

Mercedes turned toward Michelle and peeled back her lips. Her gums had been bleeding and the inside of her lips were cut. He had punched her so hard Michelle could see the indentions of her teeth on the inside of her lips.

"Are your teeth loose?" Michelle asked.

Mercedes shook her head carefully. "No, they are just sore, too," she replied.

"He's a coward, hitting you like that." She said angrily.

"I don't think he's a coward. I think he's crazy. We just need to listen to what he says so we can avoid him doing anything else to us," Mercedes replied.

"Exactly what I was thinking."

Mercedes hesitated for a moment. Then she asked in a small voice, "Were my parents looking for me?"

Michelle nodded vehemently. "Yeah, the whole town has been looking. They held a press conference at the gym, and there were a lot of people there. They've also been playing it a lot on the news."

The two continued to talk throughout the night, coming up with a plan of action: what they would and wouldn't do in order to keep the monster from going on one of his crazy rants. They also talked about what they would do once they were found and brought back home. Given the situation, they still remained hopeful that one day soon they would be found.

With the car ride so short after being abducted they both knew they were still in the immediate area of Briscoe and played the guessing game with each other about what building they might be in. Time seemed to stand still with them unable to see if it was night or day outside. The room they were trapped in shut out from the light with no windows at all.

"So, do you have any idea who this guy might be?" Michelle asked finally.

"No," Mercedes replied. "With his mask on his voice is muffled, and he's always wearing that suit with the gloves. I can't even tell what race he is."

"Well I guess it's better that we don't know what he looks like. If we knew, then we would be able to possibly identify him; if he knew we could identify him then he definitely wouldn't be letting us go."

The two went to the north wall and sat down, positioning themselves side by side between the wall and the table. They had never met before but were now relying on each other for support. They continued talking until they had both fallen back to sleep. All they could do now was wait, wait and see what would come next from the evil man who was keeping them hidden.

CHAPTER 8

Captain Cruz sat in the chair in front of Caldwell's desk, watching Caldwell pace back and forth. Caldwell had informed him about the kidnapper's call and asked him to come down for more details. He was too agitated to sit as he debriefed the captain.

"OK, so yesterday I got a call on my office phone from a guy claiming to be the kidnapper, who said he had both girls. I called Gabe and Logan from the IT department and had them put a bug on my phone just in case he called back. They got here this morning and got the phone tap set up. Well, it wasn't long after that I got a call from the same guy."

"How do you know it was the same guy?"

"His voice sounded the same, but the thing that threw me off was that this guy already knew about me having a tap on my phone."

"Wait, how did he know that?" Captain Cruz asked with a puzzled look on his face.

"I asked myself the exact same thing. So, after the second phone call I called the guys from IT to come back to my office and check the machine again. That's when they told me the call had been placed from a phone in our department building."

"Do you still have the recording?"

"Yes, look, I'll show you," Caldwell said eagerly.

Captain Cruz followed him to the side computer where the data from the phone tap had been recorded. Before the IT guys had left, Gabe had shown him how to use the equipment so that he wouldn't have to call them the next time he got a phone call.

"OK, listen to this." Caldwell pressed play, and the audio recording began.

"Look, that's where it was able to trace the call back to our department."

Captain Cruz looked down at the computer monitor and saw the address posted in red bold letters: *Call made from: 704 Lonestar St. Briscoe, Texas.*

The recording stopped playing, but Captain Cruz was still looking at the computer screen.

"Wait, what did he say about the sand is flowing?"

"I don't know. I guess he's using that as his calling card. He wrote it on the letters, remember, and he has said it each time he has called."

"Hmmmm, I wonder what he means by that."

"No telling with this guy; he is obviously not all there."

"Careful who you insult, Detective. Often these guys have genius-caliber minds. They just chose to use them for bad instead of good."

"So, what are we going to do about the calls coming from our own building?" Caldwell asked.

"Well, Detective, it's going to be hard getting the info for everyone in this building, we have so many smaller departments that operate out of here. We can start by getting a roster. From there we will have an officer from one of our patrol units man the front door. He will log in everyone who comes into the station with their name, date, and time. When they leave he will sign them out with the time they left; that way we know who was here and at what times. How does that sound?"

"It's worth a shot, but make sure none of these guys know the reason why we are doing this."

"It's OK, Detective. I'll send out an email that we are going to be monitoring time at the mayor's request for the month of October. Is there any way this guy could have made the call from somewhere else and it appear like it came from here?"

"Yes sir, sounds like a plan. Well it's highly unlikely, this guy would have to be really good with computers to pull that off."

Captain Cruz left, saying that he would be implementing the log-in, log-out procedures immediately. Caldwell knew it was a good plan. If whoever had made the call tried it again, it would be a lot easier to single them out by cross-referencing them with the entry roster. For now he would obtain a roster of the buildings employees and the shifts they worked. He couldn't omit the possibility of staff other than cops making the calls.

It was Thursday and had been two days since Michelle was kidnapped, and they had received no other calls or tips. Mercedes parents had gone back to their day-to-day work lives because they couldn't afford to miss any longer. They were not talking and were living at separate addresses. The local news continued to post stories about the missing girls, urging the public to contact the Briscoe Sheriff's Department with any leads and advising parents to accompany their children when they went out.

Detective Caldwell was back in his office, still trying to narrow down the sex offender list. He was down to only five people; his next step would be to interview those five. It was a quarter to eight at night when the office phone rang. His heart immediately began to race, and he felt his palms get sweaty. It rang again, and he reached down and picked up the phone.

"Detective Caldwell speaking."

"Hey there, Detective, you didn't think I had forgotten about you, did you?"

He pushed the receiver closer to his ear while leaning forward towards his desk.

"Why would I think that?" Caldwell responded.

"Well, it's been two long days, and I've seen you walking around like somebody shot your dog. I have a question. Do you plan on retiring soon?"

"Why would I be retiring?"

"Well, I know the stress of this case seems to be taking a toll on you. What's the public going to think about you when you can't figure anything out about not just one but two missing teenage girls?"

"It doesn't matter what they think. I'm sure they know I'm doing my best."

The line was quiet and for a second he thought that the kidnapper had hung up. "Hello? Hello?"

"I'm still here, Detective. I want to make a deal with you."

"What kind of a deal?"

"I'll let these girls go if you go on the news and admit that you can't find these girls and that you are retiring from the agency."

"Hell, no," he responded knowing the kidnapper probably wouldn't honor his side of the deal.

"That says a lot about your character, Detective."

"Like what?"

"That you would pick your ego and pride over two girls."

"You can't say that, you piece of shit."

"I did say that, because it's something that would be so easy to do. Well, think about my offer. I got to be going now. Don't forget, the sand is flowing."

The kidnapper hung up the phone. Detective Caldwell instantly paced to the computer that had been monitoring the calls. Clicking the scan button, he waited. Again, it took the software a little over five minutes to process the call, and the computer finally beeped, showing the results.

He couldn't believe his eyes: the address was posted in red bold letters.

Call made from: 704 Lonestar St. Briscoe, Texas.

He had made another call from inside the police department building. Remembering that the log-in officer was posted at the front door, Caldwell ran out of his office and into the elevator. When the doors came open on the first floor, he hurried to the officer posted at the door.

"Where is your log?" he asked.

"What log?" the officer asked.

"The one you're supposed to be using to log everyone in and out at the front door. Isn't that why you are here?"

Caldwell knew he had come off as an asshole, but he could feel the pressure, the race against time.

"We ran out of room on the logs; they were all filled up."

Detective Caldwell brought his hands to his face. "Oh my God, I can't believe this, oh my God, oh my God! Are you not smart enough to make more copies of the log before using the last one, you idiot?"

"I thought I wasn't supposed to leave my duty post, sir," said the officer stiffly, clearly offended.

"Well, what the hell is the point of you having a duty post if you're not doing your assigned job?"

"I was going to tell you I have been writing the times and names of the people right here."

The officer lifted the piece of paper with names and times written in pen. Detective Caldwell had an uneasy sick feeling in his stomach. He had just treated this officer like a child, called him names, and spoken to him like he didn't matter.

"I'm sorry, I'm so sorry . . . just . . ."

"It's OK, Detective, I understand," the officer said, handing him the paper.

As Caldwell looked at the list of names, he saw only two that had not been logged out. One was Derick, another of the guys from the IT department, and the other was the dispatcher on duty.

He gave the officer back the piece of paper and turned around as he heard the ding from the elevator. Slowly he raised his right hand to his sidearm. The doors opened, and Captain Cruz walked out of the elevator toward them at the exit door.

Detective Caldwell turned to look at the officer and then back at Captain Cruz.

"Wait a minute," he said to himself.

He turned back and grabbed the log from the table. Scanning the names, he found Captain Cruz's. His eyes scanned the paper to the section labeled *Log Out*. Next to the captain's name was the time of 6:30 p.m.

He turned back around and was now facing Captain Cruz.

"Wait, wait, wait, what are you doing here?"

Cruz gave him a puzzled smile. "I forgot the charger to my duty cell phone and I had to come back and grab it."

"Why aren't you logged in on the log?"

"I told the officer I was just going to run up and get the charger really quick."

"Oh, so these log-in and log-out rules don't apply to you? Just because you're the captain means you think you can do whatever you want? How do I know that's what you were here doing?"

"Listen here, Detective, what are you trying to say?" Cruz asked, reaching into his pocket and pulling out the charger. "I suggest you watch what you're saying before you end up on suspension."

The elevator made another ding, and Derick from the IT department stepped out and started walking to the exit.

"What were you doing here?" Detective Caldwell asked him.

"I was here finishing up some work on a new computer program we're developing. Oh, and the captain stopped in to ask me a few questions about the bug on your phone."

Caldwell turned to look at Captain Cruz then back toward Derick.

"Oh, did he now? I thought he was just here grabbing his charger, but I guess he thought he had time to stop on the second floor to visit your department and talk, right?"

Caldwell looked back at Cruz, who was now clearly upset with his behavior.

"Damnit, Detective, that's enough!" he thundered.

But before Caldwell could respond, sirens in the building started going off. They all covered their ears attempting to muffle the sound of the alarm.

"What the hell is that?" Cruz yelled.

The officer had left the desk positioned by the front door.

"It's the fire exit alarm." He continued to the wall behind the front desk where there was a flashing red light on a monitor. "It's this one," he said and took off running down the hallway.

Captain Cruz, Derick from IT, and Detective Caldwell all followed behind him. Turning once they got to the end of the long hallway, they could see the fire exit door still wide open; someone else had been in the building. Whoever it was now was gone.

CHAPTER 9

THE SOUND OF the sliding doors woke them from their sleep. Michelle and Mercedes scrambled to their feet while still trying to remember where they were. Sleep was an escape from the reality of the situation they were in, and now they had returned to the nightmare they were living.

The inner sliding door flew open, and *he* stepped inside quickly, sliding the door shut behind him. He had changed his suit; he was now wearing khaki slacks with a white shirt and red tie covered by a blue vest. The mask was still the same though.

One thing the girls had both noticed was no matter where he was or what clothes he was wearing, he always had on black leather gloves. He was careful not to leave any evidence behind.

He was carrying two plastic bags and reached out, giving one to Mercedes.

"Here are the clothes I got you. I didn't know your size, so I just got you medium."

Mercedes took the bag. She opened it and reached inside, pulling out black sweats and a black hoodie.

The kidnapper walked to the table and set down the other bag. Stepping back, he looked at Michelle and pointed to the bag.

"There are two blankets in there, one for each of you."

"Thank you," she said.

He reached into his pocket and pulled out his phone. The screen lit up, and he made his way to one of the chairs and sat down, making sure he was in a position where he could keep his eye on both girls.

Mercedes had taken the clothes and walked back to the dark corner where she had been when she used Michelle's hoodie for a cover. Michelle had turned to keep her eyes on him; she saw that he was now looking directly at Mercedes. She thought, *This pervert is trying to catch a glimpse of her while she's changing.* He kept his eyes fixed in her direction until she had put on both the hoodie and the sweats. When she turned around, he turned his attention back to his phone and used his thumb to navigate the screen.

Michelle was still looking at him. She wondered, *What does he look like under that mask? Does he smile when he does the horrible things he does? Is it the devil himself?*

"So, there's good news for you two," he said. "It says here they have extended the search for you two to an additional thirteen counties and they are also looking at bringing in the FBI. The Texas Rangers have also started to look at the case."

He clicked the screen and put the phone back into his pocket, then grabbed a radio clipped to his belt and turned it on. "It looks like this thing will come in handy after all."

"Do you have our cell phones?" Mercedes asked.

"Yeah, I have them, but they are turned off right now."

"Do you think you could let us speak to our parents, just to let them know we are OK?"

He angled his head to the side, and Michelle knew that he was considering allowing them to call.

"Please?" Michelle asked. "It won't hurt just to let us talk to them."

"I'm not that dumb. I know that any activity from the phones can be tracked to a general location using the service tower the phones are connected to when they are on. Sorry to break it to you, but I also think that the FBI getting involved isn't likely."

He stood up from his chair, walked over to the table, and pulled out the top drawer. "Let's make this a little more interesting," he said. "I'll allow each of you to send four messages apiece."

Michelle sighed. "Thank you, thank you so much."

"Wait," he said. "The way this is going to work is you're going to tell me what to write and I'll send it for you. When I get a response, I'll allow you to answer back. Understood?"

Michelle had hung her head down after hearing him say that he would be the one to send the messages. She thought to herself, *At least I'll get to let them know I'm alive if I do this.*

"OK, I'll do it," she said.

"What about you?" he asked looking in the direction of Mercedes.

"Yeah, that's fine. I'll do it too."

He turned their phones on, and the bright screens lit up. He knew it wouldn't be long before they knew where he was. His plan would soon fall into place.

"OK, who is going first?"

"She can go," Michelle said without hesitation. Mercedes had been gone a few days longer and had also been raped by the masked man. She felt that Mercedes deserved to make the first call.

"OK, who is it that you want me to send your message to?"

"My mom."

"What is it you want to tell her?"

"Just say that I'm OK and that I love her."

They watched as he scrolled through the contacts, clicked on Mom, and selected the option for a message to be sent. Then he typed in the message, and the phone made a swoosh sound as he sent it.

"OK, the first one is gone," he said.

It hadn't even been a minute before the phone dinged with an incoming message. Looking down at the screen, he read the message out loud.

"She said thank God and not to worry, that everyone is working hard to bring you home."

"Next message?"

"Tell her again that I love her and to tell Dad that I'm OK and that I miss him."

"Oh, about that, your parents are kind of on a little break."

"What do you mean, they are on a break?" Mercedes asked.

"Well, remember you told me about your mom's friend Sam and how she was meeting up with him?"

She cut him off before he could finish.

"You told my dad about her doing that?" She closed her eyes and tears appeared in the corners. "Why the hell would you do that?" she asked.

"Oh, I didn't tell him; I told the cops, the news. They all got a letter with her juicy information." He started to laugh. "I want to humiliate your mother for being stupid."

"Shut up, you asshole, don't you realize you're destroying my family? And for what, is this just a little game to you?"

She knew she had screwed up again, but she couldn't help it. She was tired of the game he was playing. All too quickly she remembered what had happened last time she had talked back to him.

Before she could apologize, he slammed the phone on the floor, where it shattered into pieces. Mercedes screamed in anger, and he pushed her, causing her to fly backward. Her back hit against the wall, and he followed, grabbing her by the shoulders and pinning her against the wall.

He angled his body, making sure he wouldn't take a kick or a knee to his groin.

"Look, bitch, it wasn't me that was out there cheating on your dad, was it?"

Mercedes had turned her head against the inside of her left shoulder and was looking down. She didn't want to be hit again.

"Was it?" he screamed, punching the wall beside her head.

When she didn't respond, he grabbed her by the arms and threw her to the ground.

"Hey!" Michelle screamed, which got his attention.

"You see what she did?" he shouted at her. "She is the reason you won't be getting to contact your family."

The initial thought brought the blood rushing to her face. She couldn't help but to be mad at Mercedes. The two of them had already talked about Mercedes not losing her cool and talking back to him. Now her actions had cost Michelle her chance to send messages her family.

He stormed to the exit door, mumbling cuss words under his breath. He slid the door open and slung it back closed behind him. Michelle ran to the door, where she could hear him securing the chain that held it closed. Looking through a small hole in the metal door, she was able to see him. He turned, walking to the other door, but before he opened it he took off the mask setting it on a chair beside the door.

She could see the back of his head and had a partial view of the left side of his face. His hair was clean cut and light brown. He had no facial hair, and his skin tone was fair.

She kept her eyes fixed on the man, hoping he would turn around while closing the door and give her more details to go by. But he had already started sliding the door shut before she got a chance to see.

"I'm sorry," Mercedes said.

Michelle turned to look at her. Mercedes was still lying on the ground. Her eyes were red and her cheeks still shiny from tears.

When Michelle didn't respond, Mercedes told her again.

"Look, I'm sorry, Michelle. I know we talked about me cooperating with him, but I'm not going to just let—"

Michelle cut her off midsentence. "I don't want to hear your shit right now. I'm tired of you putting both of us at risk because of your pride about your mom. I mean, he is right, isn't he? Your mom shouldn't have been doing what she was doing anyway . . . right?"

Before Mercedes could respond, Michelle walked off. She didn't want to hear anything else Mercedes had to say.

CHAPTER 10

D ETECTIVE CALDWELL SPENT the rest of the night apologizing to Captain Cruz for his behavior in the lobby a few hours earlier. Captain Cruz was understanding about the situation and sat down with him to talk about the two cases.

"Look, Marc, I have known you a long time and I know you are good at what you do, but I'm beginning to think this may be a little too much for you, you dealing with this type of criminal and working on both cases."

These words Detective Caldwell did not want to hear, and he was quick to respond.

"No, Captain, I have a handle on this. It's not too much for me, it's just . . . it's just . . . I don't want to let this asshole win. He is not going to beat me. I will find these girls and bring them home."

He didn't want to be humiliated any further and was becoming blind to the fact that his ego was playing such a negative role in the case.

"Marc, I want to believe you. I'm just beginning to think you have too much on your plate right now. I mean, talking to me earlier, it was like you were thinking I had something to do with this whole thing. Why don't you hand over one of the cases to Shawn? He has lots of experience also, and maybe two minds working on the case will work better than one."

The words made Caldwell's stomach turn. He felt that allowing someone else to work the case with him would be a slap in the face. He would forever think that he wasn't good enough to solve the case alone.

"Captain, please just trust me on this. Give me a few more days to get something together, and if I don't have a direction this case is moving toward by then, you can hand over one of the cases to Shawn."

Cruz was quiet for a moment, and Caldwell could almost see the wheel spinning in his head as he was thinking.

"OK, Marc, I'll let you continue, but if you have any more of this outrageous behavior I won't hesitate to put Shawn in charge of this whole thing. Do you understand, Detective?"

"Yes sir," Caldwell replied.

Cruz left, closing the door behind him. The talk had Caldwell feeling a little discouraged. He went to the personal shrine of plaques and certificates hanging from his wall. Grabbing one, he took a swipe, wiping off the thin layer of dust that covered it.

Briscoe, Texas Officer of the Year
Detective Marc Caldwell

Thank you for the hard work, dedication, persistence, and courage you put into every day you serve our community.

He smiled, hanging the plaque back in place. That was enough to put his mind back where it needed to be. *I just need to put in a little more effort,* he thought to himself. He went to his desk, looking at the list of names he had narrowed the search down to. Flipping the page, he went over the list of leads that he had received. Cross-referencing them with the facts in the case, he narrowed down the leads. Then it hit him: Why had he not been thinking about this the whole time? The person who had taken the girls was still here somewhere in this town.

Picking up the phone, he called Captain Cruz cell phone.

"What's up, Marc?"

"Hey, Captain, I was just calling to get your authorization to set up roadblocks leaving town. The person who took the girls has to still be here in town. He made the calls from our office and had to be here earlier. I hate it but like it at the same time. I figure if we set up blocks on the main roads leaving town, we can at least keep the kidnapper from leaving with the girls."

"Sure, that works for me. I'll call Sergeant Alvarez who is in charge of street patrol and get him started on that."

Caldwell smiled to himself. "I appreciate it, Captain." He had barely set the office phone down when his cell phone began to ring.

"Hello, Detective Marc Caldwell speaking."

"Detective Caldwell, it's Laura Vargas, Mercedes's mother." He could tell from the sound of her voice that she had been crying. "I got a text from Mercedes's phone."

"What? When was this?" he asked.

"About five minutes ago."

"Why are you letting me know now?"

"I'm sorry, Detective. I called José to let him know about the text, and to tell him I would be calling you."

"What all did she say?"

"The messages only said that she was OK and that she loved me and for me to tell her dad she loved him."

"Are you at home right now?"

"Yes, I'm here. José is already here too."

"Well, stay there. I'm fixing to head that way, and I'll look at the messages myself."

"OK, Detective, thank you."

He hung up the phone and grabbed the two files from the desk. He folded the papers with his notes and list of sex offenders and put them into his pocket. Back in the lobby, he talked to the officer who had been working the front door.

"Hey, Detective, they weren't able to get any prints off the fire exit door."

"OK, are you the only one stationed here?"

"No sir, Captain called for another officer to come down to the station so constant rounds could be made in the building. It's Officer Ramirez; he went ahead and locked all the doors leading to the stairs so that the only way up or down is through the elevator."

"OK, well, I'm going to be heading out for a bit. You two be safe."

"Yes sir, Detective, you too."

He wrote down his exit time and walked out of the front door. It was already 12:30 a.m.; the past week seemed to be flying, and he was tired. The talk Captain Cruz had given him was a little more than a boost of energy; he had made the case a personal one with the jokes and tricks the kidnapper had been playing. He was determined to find him for the sake of his ego, the safety of the girls, and for the peace of mind of their parents. That was enough to keep him going.

He grabbed his cell phone and dialed Detective Peterson.

"What's up, Marc?"

"Hey, bro, are you asleep?"

"Nah, I was just here at my house watching TV, and thinking about the cases."

"Well, you want to meet me at the Vargas house? Laura, Mercedes's mother . . . she called and told me she got a text from Mercedes's phone."

"What, are you serious?"

"Yeah, you want to meet me over there?"

"Sure, bro, let me put on my boots and I'll meet you there."

"OK, that'll work. See you in a bit."

"OK, bye."

Caldwell hung up the phone and turned on the radio. The Texas country song "Shut Up and Dance" was playing. He turned up the dial and sang along to the lyrics, at the same time wondering about the text messages that had been sent from Mercedes's phone. Surely this guy knew that the authorities could pinpoint the calls to a certain area. He had to have known a lot because he had managed to stay one step ahead this entire time. It had to be just another part of the games he had been playing.

The song was finishing as he pulled up to the Vargas house. Just as he was about to get out of the car, the radio DJ came on.

"That one right there was a special request. Mercedes Vargas, your friends are out here thinking about you. They said that was your favorite song and requested it. Let's hope . . ."

Caldwell turned off the car and got out, slamming the door behind him. The radio DJ was a bitter reminder of the fact they still hadn't found her. He could see the inner wooden door open and several cars parked in the driveway. As he was getting to the Vargases front door, moving headlights reflected off the house. He stopped and waited as Peterson parked his car and walked up to meet him.

"That was fast, bro," Caldwell said.

"Come on, you know I got you. We are going to get this asshole, right?" Peterson said, starting to smile.

Detective Caldwell smiled back. "Yeah, the hounds are on his heels. He better be scared."

Mrs. Vargas had made her way to the outer glass door and opened it, waving the two detectives inside.

Caldwell said, "Good evening, Mr. and Mrs. Vargas. This is my coworker, Detective Shawn Peterson. He has been assisting me with Mercedes's case and the case with Michelle Foster, the other girl who has been taken."

"It's good to see you, Detectives," she said in a relieved but shaken voice. "Did you want to see the messages?" Mrs. Vargas asked, handing him the phone with the screen already on the conversation.

Caldwell read the messages and gave the phone to Peterson. "Have you heard anything else since receiving the messages?" he asked Mrs. Vargas.

"No, I tried to call her phone, but it went straight to voice mail." She said anxiously.

Detective Peterson spoke up. "How long were you texting back and forth?"

"Just a couple of minutes, long enough to receive those messages."

Peterson looked at Caldwell. "We should set up a trace on that phone."

"Do you think it was enough for a hit?"

"Yeah, as long as messages went to and from that phone, we should have something."

Caldwell turned to Mrs. Vargas. "That's our next option. We should have a location within a mile radius of where those texts were sent."

"Oh, thank God," she said as she started to cry. Mr. Vargas had now gotten out of his chair and started to comfort his wife.

"First thing in the morning we will start a cell phone trace," Caldwell continued. "We would start one right now but the equipment we normally use has come up missing and we will now need the assistance from a third party."

Mr. Vargas answered, "Yes sir, yes sir, thank you very much."

"We're going to get going now. We'll let you know when we hear something new. Call us immediately if you get any more messages."

"Yes sir, yes sir," Mr. Vargas said again.

"Thank you, Detectives," Mrs. Vargas said, wiping the tears from her face.

CHAPTER 11

H E SAW DETECTIVE Caldwell and Peterson walking out of the front door to the house and turned on his headlights. He had followed Caldwell from the station and had stopped far enough down the street that the detective wouldn't see that he had been followed. Once the two detectives had went inside, he had pulled his car a little closer.

It was a rush to him, playing cat and mouse, and with them not being able to catch him so far, he had grown cockier. He knew the reason they had been there; the mother had called them after getting the text messages from her daughter's phone. He smiled; they were in a game of chess and he felt he was a few moves ahead. In fact, he knew he had been ahead the entire time.

Just as he was passing the house, he turned on the interior lights and eased off the gas pedal while rolling down the passenger side window. He saw both detectives looking at his car. They turned to look at each other then back to the car. He was wearing a yellow ski mask that had a smiling face painted on it, the mask grabbed their attention. With his heart rate increasing he screamed can't catch me and stepped on the gas, causing the tires to screech as he sped off.

Both detectives ran to their cars and got inside. Starting them, they sped off after him. He knew they were thinking this was finally their chance to get him. *Damn it*, he thought to himself as he took turn after turn, making sure they wouldn't catch up to him.

The detectives continued heading north, not knowing that the first thing that he had done was turn around and had started heading south. One of the oldest tricks in the book was going to save him this time. He still had the police scanner he had taken from the station and was using it to aid in his escape.

He laughed to himself at the sound of their frantic voices. *These cops are amateurs*, he thought.

He brought his speed back down to the legal limit. The only way he was going to get caught now would be by another mistake on his part; avoid any traffic violations and he was home free. It didn't take long for him to reach the hiding place where the two girls had been stashed. He pulled into the back of the abandoned building, where there was a section that had been closed off by a cinder block wall about eight feet high. Since no one had kept up with the place, the wall had been overtaken with vines and small trees. It was the perfect hiding place. You weren't going to see anything there unless you had actually went looking. He listened to the scanner and heard the car sirens, they had gone clear across town; he was safe.

———

When the two detectives met back at the station later that night, they were angry at how the kidnapper had beaten them again.

"How in the hell could we have let him get away?" Caldwell said.

Peterson followed him toward the entrance of the building. "That son of a bitch is brave; he's been watching us the whole time. Have you ever seen that car before?"

"I don't know. I haven't really been paying attention to notice if anyone has been following me."

"Me either."

They entered the police station, where there was a new officer posted at the front door.

"How are you today, Officer"—Caldwell had never seen the cop before but glancing down at his name tag he could see the name—"Camacho?"

"I'm good, sir. Can you please sign in for me?"

There was a new sheet that had started over at midnight, and the form was blank. He wrote Detective Peterson and himself down with an entry time of 3:30 a.m.

Man, the time is flying by, he thought as they entered the elevator. When they reached the office floor, Detective Peterson headed off to the break room.

"I'm going to make us some coffee."

"OK, sounds good," Caldwell said, heading to his office. He opened the door to the familiar scent of Hawaiian breeze he had in his candle melt. "Home sweet home," he said, putting the files back on his desk.

"Shawn!" he shouted impatiently. He needed that coffee.

"Hold on, dude, I'm coming." Peterson walked into the office carrying two cups. "You know you can't rush perfection."

"I know, I know," Caldwell said with a smile.

"What do you think we should do?" Detective Peterson asked.

"Well, there isn't a lot we can do right now; he got away. Yeah, he was driving a dark blue, maybe black car, but that's all we know right now. We'll just have to wait a few more hours until we can get a trace on the location of that cell phone."

———◆———

Back at the abandoned building, the kidnapper had already put on his mask and entered the room where Mercedes and Michelle were still not talking.

"Aww, what happened here? Are we mad at each other?" he taunted, laughing to himself. "OK, you two, get over here and sit down."

The girls got up from where they had been sitting on the floor and made their way to their seats in the middle of the room. He walked to the table, where there were only two bottles of water left.

"Mercedes, come here."

She didn't move at first, causing him to turn around.

"Are you still going to be that way? You don't get tired of me beating your ass, do you? Get up out of that chair before I come drag you over here."

Michelle reached over, pushing Mercedes by the arm.

"Just go," she said.

Mercedes jerked, pulling her shoulder back, then turning to give Michelle a go-to-hell look. She got up and walked over to where he was standing. The light shining on her revealed the bruises on her face and arms. Her lip was split and bloody, and her hair clumped together from where it hadn't been washed in over a week. Looking in her eyes, he knew she had been broken. The terror he had caused was over for now, but the memories would be something she would live with for the rest of her life.

"Look, I'm going to let you go in the morning. I don't want you thinking that me taking you was your fault, because it wasn't, but your actions once we got here may have caused some issues."

Michelle had been eavesdropping on what he was telling Mercedes and now spoke up in desperation.

"Are you going to let me go, too? Please let me go; I won't say anything, just please."

"Why is that hole in your face moving?" he snapped. "Will you please shut up? Can you do that?"

Michelle turned the other direction and got quiet.

"OK, good!" He focused his attention back on Mercedes. The look on her face said it all; she wanted him to let Michelle go, too. He leaned forward, whispering in her ear, "I'm going to let her go, too. I don't want you two anymore . . . I've proven my point, OK?"

He pulled back, and Mercedes nodded her head yes. "OK, go sit down."

He thought of the options he had. Since he had used Mercedes phone to send the texts, it wouldn't be long until the whole police force was surrounding the abandoned building, here to find the one who had shaken up the town over the past week and to get their victims back. He had sent the text messages from Mercedes's phone on purpose; he knew they would trace the messages and get a general location of where he was. *But they needed my help*, he thought. The game wasn't fun if they didn't give him a little bit of a challenge.

He still had the police scanner but to preserve the battery he would need to use it only when necessary. For the next couple of hours, he could plan the way the rest of this would turn out. He didn't want to get caught, of course; he knew he would get more time in prison for kidnapping than he would if he had killed someone.

He looked at his watch; it was 4:15 a.m.

"OK, ladies, let's get this party started."

CHAPTER 12

W ITH THE THOUGHT of going home on their minds, Michelle and Mercedes willingly helped clean the building that had been used to hold them hostage, gathering the pieces of torn tape from around the chairs and off the floor.

"Don't forget your pants," Michelle said.

Mercedes walked over to the corner where she had left them, picking them up; they were still wet and had begun to smell. She took everything and tossed it into a black bag. The initial thought of peeing on herself embarrassed her, but inside she knew there was nothing she could have done to prevent that. Even if she had been awake, she'd been tied to a chair, unable to move at all. Michelle picked up the blankets and grabbed the trash from the table. They put all of the smaller bags into two separate but larger trash bags and set them beside the sliding door.

"OK," the kidnapper told them, "the way this is going to work is, Mercedes, I'm going to let you go. I want you to go directly to the police station and tell them who you are and where you were being kept. Michelle, I'm going to keep you here with me."

"But why?" Michelle asked with a worried look on her face.

"I can't let both of you go right now; you two will get to the police too fast, and I won't have time to get away."

Michelle was unsure of this but went along with what he said. At least he hadn't killed them. "OK," she replied.

The kidnapper continued: "Mercedes, when you get there you also need to make sure that you tell them that Michelle will be here, OK?"

"OK," she replied.

Back at the station Caldwell and Peterson had taken turns napping over the past few hours. It wasn't a lot of sleep they would be running on, but it would have to work.

The moment the clock hit 9:00 a.m., they got in touch with the company that would be completing the cell phone trace.

Caldwell had attached a map of the city to the board on the wall, right under the girls' names. It took a little over thirty minutes for the trace to come back, giving them a one-mile radius of where they could be. The news was good; the text had been placed in a neighborhood in the northeast division of the city, which meant Mercedes and Michelle were still in Briscoe.

Captain Cruz had called an emergency briefing in order to come up with the crews that would be assisting with the search.

———

Back at the abandoned building, everything had been gathered up.

"Go ahead and leave the roll of tape on the chair," said the kidnapper. "I'm going to drop off Mercedes about fifteen blocks from the station. As soon as she gets out, we will come back here, where I will tape you to the chair and leave. As long as you both cooperate, this is going to all end today, OK?"

Both girls nodded yes. He pulled a gun out from his pocket. "OK, 'cause if you don't I will shoot you both."

"We agree," Mercedes said with Michelle adding, "Yeah, we agree."

This was the first time since taking them that he had even shown a gun, but the girls knew not to test him.

He unlocked the first door and slid it open.

"Get the trash," he said, pointing at the bags they had left by the door.

They grabbed the bags and entered the hallway between the two doors.

"Oh, I almost forgot," he said, turning around and walking back into the room. He was only gone a second before coming back.

"Did you forget to grab your hourglass?" Michelle asked.

"Nah, that was already here. I'm not going to take what isn't mine." He laughed under his breath.

Leading the way, he opened the second door, which revealed a long hallway. They started to walk, then made a left turn that led them down another hallway.

After making the turn, the girls could see the light from outside shining in through the exit door. They both smiled, knowing that freedom was only a few feet away. When they reached the exit, he opened the door and they followed him to the car that had been parked behind the wall.

Mercedes tried to look at the license plate, but with him so close she couldn't get a clear look. He opened the trunk and they put the bags inside. Walking to the passenger side of the car, he opened the back door.

"Michelle, get in."

She lowered her head, climbing into the back seat. Before he shut the door, he reached down and turned the knob marked *Child Safety*. He walked around the back of the car, where he opened the driver's side rear door and activated the child safety lock on it, then shut the door.

Reaching into his pocket, he pulled out his gun and pointed it at Mercedes.

"Get in the car," he said.

She didn't hesitate.

"Buckle your seatbelt. Michelle, put yours on, too." He was taking every precaution to make sure that they didn't get out of the car earlier than he wanted.

Mercedes was trying to remember every detail about the car without being too obvious. It was dark blue, and she saw the Mercedes Benz logo appear on the radio screen after he turned the car on.

He reached down to the cupholder where the police scanner was sitting and turned it on. Mercedes had followed his hand movements to the radio, but there was something else had caught her eye. There was a police badge sitting in the console where people normally kept spare change. Lifting her head back straight, she tried to read the information on it through the corner of her eye, but then he told her to put her head down between her knees and keep it there until he said she could pick it back up.

———

He pulled the car onto the street. The black ice that had covered the roads was starting to melt with the sun getting higher in the sky. The clock read 10:15 a.m., and he knew the police had already gotten started on their phone trace.

The sand is flowing, he thought as he smiled to himself.

CHAPTER 13

AFTER GETTING TO the area of town he thought would be safest to drop Mercedes off, the kidnapper pulled over to the side of the curb.

"Take your shoes off and give them to me," he demanded.

She reached down and untied them, then handed them to him one by one.

"All right, you are free to go," he said.

She opened the car door and unbuckled her seat belt. Twisting sideways, she pushed her feet out of the car and onto the cold ground. The ice felt like fire. She picked them back up quickly before putting them down again. The ground was cold enough that it took her breath away. She felt the cold not only in her feet but all the way through her body. It was like she had jumped into a swimming pool filled with ice water.

Climbing the rest of the way out, she shut the door behind her and hurried off down the sidewalk. She smiled, knowing that she was free but still hesitant, not knowing if this was another one of his sick games. Would he allow her to think she was free and then turn back around and force her into the car like he had the night this nightmare had begun?

The car sped off behind her, and she didn't bother to look at which direction he was heading. The freezing sidewalk was the only thing on her mind. *Mind over matter, mind over matter*, she kept repeating in her head, but it was too much. She stopped and sat down on the back steps of Debbie's Downtown Diner. She thought for a second about trying to go inside, but quickly changed her mind. *What if he was still watching from a distance*, she thought. Reaching down, she rubbed her feet; they were frozen to the touch. She knew that she had to hurry; as cold as it was, it wouldn't be long before her feet got frostbite. For some reason, the scene from the movie *Mr. Deeds* popped into her head, the part where the nephew showed the usher his black foot that had been frostbitten. She shook the thought out of her head and got moving as fast as she could down the alley. She knew running wouldn't be a good idea. There were probably still areas of black ice on the ground. With the buildings being so high and the temperature so low, the ice hadn't had time to melt.

She came to a stop again and sat down behind Garcia's Tex-Mex Diner, she lifted her feet off the ground. Looking around, she noticed a trash can with the lid half open. There was the corner of a rag sticking out; her first thought was to grab the rag and use it to cover her feet. Making her way to the can, she lifted the lid. The smell of rotting food hit her before anything, but her mind quickly returned to her freezing feet. Grabbing the rag, she discovered there was more than one, covered with what looked like old ketchup or pizza sauce. She grabbed all she could and walked back to the steps where she had been sitting. Taking the rags, she wrapped them around her feet. Too worried about the cold to think about what was smeared on them, she kept tying until they were gone.

She could see the police department in the distance and was now able to walk faster. Block by block she got closer and the smile on her face got bigger. She started to cry, knowing she had made it, she was finally there. The nightmare was over.

She made her way around the side and up to the front door, where there was still an officer posted at the door. He immediately knew who she was and opened the door to comfort her, turning to shout at the officer working the front desk to call Detective Caldwell. Picking up the phone, the officer called to the conference room on the sixth floor where she knew the detectives would be.

"Sergeant Wolven," a man answered.

"Yes, can you get me Detective Caldwell please?"

"Well, he's kind of busy; we are working on the briefings for the missing girls."

"I know, but you're never going to believe it; one of the girls just walked in."

As soon as Wolven relayed the news, Caldwell immediately rushed to the phone while everyone in the room began to stand up and talk among themselves.

"Detective Caldwell," he answered.

"Yes, Detective, one of the girls just walked in. It's Mercedes Vargas."

"I'll be right down," Caldwell said, hanging up the phone. "Hey, guys, go ahead and start getting your equipment ready; we may have to be leaving sooner than I thought."

Caldwell walked out of the conference room and headed to the elevator. As he pushed the down arrow, it seemed like it took years for the doors to open.

He reached the first floor, the elevator door opened, and there she was. A group of officers were huddled around her; one of them had taken off his duty jacket and draped it over her, trying to keep her warm.

As Caldwell got closer, the sight of her face made him cringe; both of her eyes were black, and her nose looked possibly broken, too. Her top lip was split, and both her arms had minor scrapes and bruises. She had tears in her eyes and was asking for her parents. There were bruises along the side of her neck and upper chest, and he could see she wasn't wearing shoes.

"OK, guys, let me talk to her."

She wiped her eyes and looked up at him.

"Mercedes, my name is Detective Caldwell. I'm so glad to see that you are alive."

"He wants you to go get Michelle," she immediately said.

"What?" Detective Caldwell asked.

"He wants you to go get Michelle, the other girl. She is in the same building where I was."

"OK, OK, what does the building look like?"

"It's the metal two story building on Lake Drive. It's the only one in that area; you shouldn't miss it."

He knew exactly what building she was talking about. In the summer months, they used the building to complete boat repairs, but during the winter the owner of the shop would leave for his cabin in Ruidoso, New Mexico. He made enough money repairing boats during the summer that he didn't have to work for the rest of the year.

"OK, guys," Caldwell said to the officers, "get her an ambulance over here right now, and get a hold of her parents. I want two officers with her at all times." He turned back around to talk to Mercedes. "They are going to take care of you, OK?"

She put her head down and started to cry.

"Nobody else is going to hurt you, I promise," he said with a lump in his throat.

He went to the front desk, where he used the phone to call the conference room on the sixth floor. Sergeant Wolven answered again.

"Hey, Sergeant, get me Detective Peterson please."

"Yes sir."

"What's up, Marc?" Peterson answered.

"Hey, go ahead and let the guys know to meet me down here; we are going to that building on the southeast side of town, the one on Lake Drive where they do the boat repair."

"Yes sir, I know what you're talking about."

"The other girl is over there, and we need to get there as quickly as possible."

"Which girl is it who showed up downstairs?"

"It's Mercedes."

"Oh, is she OK?"

"She seems to be, but she is all beat up. Get the crew down here."

"Yes sir," Peterson said, hanging up the phone.

Once everyone had gathered in the lobby, Detective Caldwell gave a briefing on what was going to happen. After giving everyone their assignments and completing a weapons check, he gave the final orders.

"I want us to be safe and effective. Remember the other girl is in that building, and I'm not sure if he will be there or not. I'm not sure if this is a set-up or what's going to happen. Keep your heads on a swivel and watch each other's backs . . . Let's go get this asshole."

The rest of the officers started to clap and cheer as they headed out of the station and to their vehicles. One by one they drove off to the southeast side of town, where they would set up in their positions surrounding the old boat factory.

While en route to the factory, Caldwell used his radio to call in all units to the immediate area. They would assist with anything that happened out of the ordinary.

Unit by unit, the officers lined up in their assigned locations until everyone was in place. The SWAT team formed a line and moved to their location outside the front door. With the point man moving to the side of the door, he gave a signal, and the second man in line, who was carrying a large sledgehammer, stepped back and with one swing struck the door where the handle had been. He then stepped back and kicked the door, causing it to fly open.

Lifting a shield in front of him the third guy in line quickly entered the building, followed by seven others. The point man and guy who kicked in the door followed behind them with weapons drawn.

The rest of the officers waited at their posts; Caldwell and Peterson along with Captain Cruz waited near the entry. The next few minutes would be a waiting game.

CHAPTER 14

IT TOOK THE team about five minutes to clear the whole building. The team leader responded over the radio.

"All units, all stations, the building is clear. I repeat, the building is clear."

Michelle was nowhere to be found.

The team exited the building one by one with the team leader being last.

"Detective Caldwell, I think you need to get over here," he said. "I think you should see something."

Caldwell and Peterson followed him as he led the way back through the building.

"The lights are on," Peterson said.

"Yeah, the owner must leave the power on over the winter months, just so he doesn't have to mess with getting it turned back during the summer," Caldwell said.

They had made a few turns and passed two sliding doors and were now in a room about twenty feet wide and twenty feet long. The room was empty except for a small metal table on the north wall. A light above the table had been left on.

"There it is," the team leader said, pointing toward the table.

Looking closer, Detective Caldwell saw it: a yellow sticky note stuck to the table. On the note was written *Maybe next time* with a smiley face drawn underneath the writing. There was also a large hourglass about a foot tall. The last of the sand from the top section was flowing to the bottom half of the timer. They had missed him by less than an hour.

"I guess that's what he was talking about when he said the sand is flowing," Peterson said.

Caldwell glared at him. "No shit, Sherlock." He was furious that the kidnapper had once again beaten him but tried to remain calm. "Did you guys find anything else?" he asked the team leader.

"No sir, my team cleared the entire building. This had to have been the room he was keeping them in. The two sliding doors had padlocks that were securing them shut. My number-two man had to use the hammer to break them off."

"OK, thanks for the help. Tell your team I said they did a damn good job."

"Yes sir, anytime. I'll make sure to tell them, sir."

Caldwell grabbed the note from the table and put it in a clear evidence bag.

"Peterson, go ahead and get forensics down here and see if they can sweep for prints or any other evidence that might link us to our guy."

"Will do, sir."

"Oh . . . and get that hourglass, too . . ." Caldwell said, walking off.

Once back in his car, he punched the steering wheel twice, causing the car to honk. The rest of the officers who had been in the area turned to see what was going on. Caldwell looked down at the radio to avoid the embarrassment. Grabbing his phone, he dialed the number to Mrs. Vargas's cell phone.

"Hello," she said.

"Mrs. Vargas, it's Detective Caldwell."

"Thank you, Detective, thank you for bringing my baby back safe."

He could tell she was trying not to cry and thought to himself, *If only I* had *brought her back. If only I had brought them both back.*

"You're welcome, Mrs. Vargas. Now when Mercedes is done at the hospital, the two officers that are with her and your family are going to bring you guys back to the station, OK?"

"Yes, Detective, is it OK if I come, too?" she asked.

"Yes, ma'am you can come. How is she doing? What have the doctors said?"

At that moment, she started to cry but quickly stopped herself in order to answer him back

"They said she is good; her nose isn't broken, just a couple of bumps and bruises, but they did say he raped her." She started to cry again.

Caldwell was speechless. He somehow felt that it was all his fault. If he had only gotten to her sooner then maybe this wouldn't have happened. For him to do something so horrible to someone who was so sweet and innocent—this wasn't a normal man they were dealing with; he was a monster.

With every part of him wanting to break down inside, he knew he had to stay strong. Stay strong for Mercedes, and her family. Stay strong for Michelle and her family. And stay strong for the case.

"I'm sorry to hear that, Mrs. Vargas, but I promise you we are going to get this guy. I'll let you go now. I'll talk to you more when you get here from the hospital."

"OK, thank you," she said before hanging up.

He now had to make a dreaded phone call to Michelle's parents. Picking up his phone, he dialed the number that Mrs. Foster had given to him at the beginning of the investigation.

"Mrs. Foster, ma'am, it's Detective Marc Caldwell. I need to talk to you. Do you have a moment?"

"Yes sir, I was just here at the house." Her voice was filled with trepidation. "What is it?"

"Well, we found Mercedes Vargas today. She showed up at the police station earlier this morning."

"Oh, that's great, Detective! What about Michelle? Can I talk to her?"

The hope and relief in her voice made him cringe. "Well, ma'am, that's what this is about. You see . . . we weren't able to get Michelle; the kidnapper still has her. Please believe me when I tell you we are doing everything in our power . . ."

Before he could finish his sentence, Mrs. Foster was crying on the other end of the line. "What . . . what do you mean, he still has her?"

"Now, ma'am, I know this is hard to hear, but I need you to calm down so that we can communicate."

The phone got silent as she tried to regain composure.

"Ma'am, I am doing all that I can to bring Michelle home. I have an interview with Mercedes

Vargas in a little while, and I'm going to get all the information I can out of her. I'll ask her how your daughter is doing and how she is being treated. I'll give you a call as soon as I find out something new, OK?"

"OK, Detective."

"Stay strong, Mrs. Foster. I promise I'm going to get your daughter back."

"OK, OK, I'll stay strong."

He hung up the phone and started the car. The drive back to the police station was a slow and agonizing one. He felt like he had lost, like he had been beaten once again. He thought to himself, *No telling where he is now.* For a moment he was filled with hope as he remembered the roadblocks he'd set up for all the roads exiting town, but then he remembered that he had radioed for all units to report to the scene for extra support.

Picking up his radio, he gave the order for all roadblock teams to report back to their locations and set up. Maybe they could get there before the kidnapper had an opportunity to slip out of town, or at least he hoped so.

Back at the station it was chaos. The local news reporters were lined up outside trying to get a story. Caldwell walked through the crowd with them pushing recorders into his face and asking about

Mercedes. They even asked about Michelle: where was she, was she alive, and was there any hope of finding her? All these questions not even he knew the answers to.

Once he was inside, the officer working the front desk told him that Captain Cruz had requested to see him.

The captain's office was on the fifth floor along with the homicide department and drug enforcement. *I wonder what captain wants this time*, he thought to himself on the elevator ride up.

The doors opened, and he stepped out. There was little traffic and it was quiet, other than a few phones ringing on the narcotics side of the floor. Captain Cruz's office was one of the first ones on the left side of the floor. Knocking twice, he got a response.

"Come in."

"Yes, Captain, you requested to speak with me?"

"Yes, go ahead and close the door and sit down."

Caldwell closed the door and sat down, waiting for Cruz to respond. The captain was typing on his computer. He had his glasses low on his nose and was glancing over them to type.

"OK, I'm done. Sorry about that. I was just trying to close this drug trafficking case."

"I understand, sir."

"So, is there anything new on the case?" Cruz asked, leaning back a little.

"No sir. I have to wait for Mercedes to get back from the hospital so I can question her a little bit about what happened."

"OK, well, I heard this asshole got away for now, but I don't want you to get discouraged. Things like this happen. We got one of the girls back and that's better than nothing, right?"

So many things were going on in Caldwell's head at that moment that he didn't know how to feel, but he agreed. "Yes sir, you're right; at least we got one of them back."

"Listen, this jerk will slip up, and when he does you'll be there to catch him. I have no doubt in my mind at all about that. That's the reason I gave you these cases to begin with was because I have faith in you and I trust you. You may have had your little mishaps, but that's water under the bridge."

"Yes sir, I know he will, but he had to have given away his position on purpose, he wanted us to know his location. This asshole is bold and he set the whole thing up. Thank you for believing in me Captain, and by the way, Detective Peterson, has been helping out a lot. I give the kid credit. He is going to be a good one once he gets a little more experience."

"Well, with him having someone like you for him to look up to and get advice from, I'm sure he will do great. Well that's all I was going to say. Keep your head up, kid, and let me know when you get your updates."

"Yes sir, will do. I just want to say again, this guy had to have set this all up."

"What do you mean he set it all up?"

"He had to have known that turning on the phones would give up his location, but he did it anyways."

"It's always hard to tell what these guys are thinking, but you may be right. Go get some rest kid."

Back in his own office, Caldwell sat down in the chair behind his desk. Leaning back, he closed his eyes.

They weren't closed long when he remembered the sticky note he had taken from the scene. Reaching into his pocket, he pulled out the evidence bag and looked at the note. "Maybe next time," he whispered to himself as he placed the bag in the center of his desk.

CHAPTER 15

AFTER A FEW hours at Lincoln Memorial Hospital, Mercedes was released and escorted to the Briscoe Police Station, where Detective Caldwell was waiting to interview her. He made sure a female officer was also present in the interview room to offer moral support and comfort if Mercedes or her mother were to need it.

"OK, Mercedes, let's start off with the day this happened. How was he able to get you into the car with him?"

"My friends had just left, and I was waiting for my mom to show up. I didn't want to be waiting at the front of the theater, so I went walking through the parking lot. I had been on the phone texting my friend Leslie when a blue car pulled up. It looked like my friend Lee's car, so I walked up to the window.

When I looked inside he already had a gun pointing right in my face. He told me not to scream or he would shoot me. Of course, I was scared and nervous. He told me to get in the car, so I opened the door and got in."

"So do you know what he looks like?"

"No, from the first time I saw him to the last time, he was wearing this creepy mask that looked like a scarecrow."

"Like a Wizard of Oz scarecrow or . . .?"

"No, this mask was evil; it had an angry, evil look to it."

"OK, what about clothes?"

"He was always dressed nice, like . . . like a banker or a businessman. He also always wore these black gloves and never took them off."

"OK, what about the kind of car it was?"

"It was either a dark blue or black Mercedes Benz."

"Good, you're doing a good job. If at any point we need to stop so we can give you a break, let me know. I'm going to try and go as fast as I can, though, so we can get out any new info about this guy."

"Thank you," she said.

"OK, once you were back at the building where he kept you two, how did he act? Did he have any mannerisms about him? Was he mean the whole time?"

"He always kept his voice concealed and was always covering his tracks. I can tell he is either smart or has been doing this a long time. He was constantly cussing and liked to taunt you and the press about what was going on. He claimed the whole reason he had taken us was to prove a point that parents have become too complacent with their children; he said parents nowadays just allow their kids to do what they want and don't expect there to be consequences."

"OK, these next few questions may be a bit difficult to answer, but just answer them the best you can, and if you need to take a break from the interview we can."

"OK," she replied.

"So your mom told me that this guy, he . . . he raped you, is that correct?"

"Yes, he tied me to a chair, and I wasn't able to move. Well, first he punched me in the face."

Mercedes began to cry, her mother took her by her shoulders and pulled her in while also beginning to tear up.

"Mercedes, we can wait a few minutes if you need it ?"

"It's ok I can continue..." She said while wiping tears from her face. "His punch knocked me out, and when I woke up, I was tied to the chair."

"So do you think that he had it in his mind the whole time that he was going to rape you?"

"I don't know. He did tell me a few times that I was really pretty and that he knew some friends who would have bought me in an instant."

"Like sell you as a prostitute?"

"No, I think he meant like a sex trafficking ring or something."

"Did he rape Michelle, too?"

"No, when she first got there he shocked her with one of those electric rods, the ones that are made for cattle. But other than that, he never touched Michelle."

"Hmmm, why do you think he only hit you?"

"I don't know . . . Well, I did talk back to him a couple of times, and he told me that if I didn't cooperate with him, he would punish me. But he said things several times that made me mad, and that's when I would act out . . . I guess I kind of brought it on myself."

"Don't say that, Mercedes. He did what he was already going to do, so don't blame yourself."

"But it's kind of true. I mean, even Michelle told me not to act out and that things would be OK. After getting shocked she did everything thing he said, and he never touched her again."

"So what happened after the rape?"

"He left the room and I stayed tied over the chair. Sometime while I was asleep I used the restroom on myself; when he got back he let Michelle loose and let her take care of me. When he came back the next time, he brought me different clothes and brought us some food."

"At what point did he let you text your mom?"

"It was last night that he let me text. He was going to let Michelle text her mom, too, but I made him mad and he wouldn't let her after that. That caused Michelle and me to get into an argument because she wanted to talk to her mom, too. After that, he came back and said he was letting me go and that Michelle would be waiting at the boat place when you guys got there.

Where is she? I want to talk to her and tell her I'm sorry I was the reason she didn't get to text her mom."

Caldwell took a drink of his coffee and was silent.

"Where is she? You guys found her, right?" Mercedes asked, alarm in her voice.

"Well, when we got there, there wasn't anyone in the room."

She was frantic. "What do you mean she wasn't there? Are you sure? Did he take her with him?"

"Mercedes, I need you to calm down."

She had started to cry again. "It's my fault, it's all my fault."

"Mercedes, there is nothing you could have done. At least you're able to help us with any information that may lead us to him."

She was crying so much now that she couldn't talk. Her mother was hugging her and had even started to cry herself.

The whole investigation was draining for everyone involved, and it took a lot for Caldwell to keep from tearing up also. It was a sad case, and he could tell she felt genuinely bad.

He said, "We are going to take a break. Feel free to step into the hallway and walk around or get something to eat or drink. I am going to my office to file these initial notes."

Fifteen minutes went by while he did this, and he made his way back to the interview room where Mercedes was with her mom, dad, and a few of her friends.

"OK," he said, getting their attention, "let's get this finished up and I can let you be on your way. Are there any more details you can give me? Try and think about small things you noticed during the whole ordeal."

Mercedes leaned back in the chair and closed her eyes; he could see the movement behind her eyelids as she replayed the final details in her mind.

"Yes, I do remember he had one of those police radios."

Caldwell took a quick look at Captain Cruz and then brought his attention back to Mercedes.

She continued, "He also had a badge."

"Wait, what? Are you sure he had a badge?" Caldwell asked.

"Yes, I'm sure, and he was always using the radio to keep up with where you guys would be searching."

"Where was the badge when you saw it?"

"It was in the center console of his car."

"Do you remember anything about it?"

She leaned back in her chair and closed her eyes again, as if she were fighting to remember every little detail about it.

"It looked exactly like yours, the same color, the same shape, the same size; it even said Briscoe Police Department on it."

Out of the corner of his eye, he could see that Captain Cruz was prompting him to finish the interview. There wasn't much more he could get from the interview; she had told him all that she could remember, and he knew she must be eager to get out of there and get home.

"OK, Mercedes, that's all I have. If for some reason you can think of anything else, anything at all, go ahead and give me a call. Your parents have my number."

"Thank you for everything, Detective Caldwell. Please try your best to find Michelle, and can you keep me updated with any new information?"

"I'll do my best, and you bet I'll let you know if I get anything new." He smiled and stood up from behind the table. Walking around to where Mercedes was, he gave her a hug. Both of her parents stepped up from their chairs and hugged him as well.

"Thank you, Detective. Thank you for everything you have done," Mercedes's mother said, and her father added, "I can't thank you enough, Detective. You helped bring my baby home."

"You're welcome. I'm glad things turned out for the best. You guys be safe now."

Caldwell still couldn't stand the fact that they were thanking him for Mercedes returning home. He felt that he had done nothing during the case but try to narrow down who it could be. The Scarecrow, as he'd come to think of the kidnapper based on Mercedes's description, letting her go was the only reason Mercedes had made it back home alive.

He made his way back to his office with Captain Cruz following behind him.

"Look, Marc, I think you have done a hell of a job. Don't let this situation bring you down; we still have Michelle to bring home. I'm going to do a count for the issued badges and see what I can find out as far as why this asshole had a badge and scanner. I'll debrief Peterson as well as to the new information Mercedes has provided."

"Are you sure, Captain?" Caldwell asked, surprised. "I can help you out with it."

"Marc . . . it's fine. Why don't you head home and get some rest? I know you need some."

The captain was right. He felt as if he hadn't slept in months, and for the past few days he had been running on fumes. Cruz gave him a pat on the back and left his office.

Caldwell walked over to the dry erase board where Mercedes's name was written and used the eraser to wipe it off. There was only one name left: Michelle Foster. Looking at the name, he still felt like he hadn't done a good job with the investigation. Walking out of the office and slowly closing the door behind him, he thought to himself, *The sand is flowing.*

CHAPTER 16

THE MONTHS THAT followed were quiet with few leads on the case at all. It was like the whole world had forgotten about Michelle Foster. Forgotten that she was still gone and that she had a mother and father at home who were still praying every night for their daughter's return.

Detective Caldwell had now turned his office into a shrine of newspaper clippings and articles on the man the media had now dubbed "the Scarecrow." A few days after leaving the police station, Mercedes had spoken with a local newspaper agency and had given them the details of the kidnapping, including the mask the kidnapper had been wearing.

Unfortunately for Mercedes, her nightmare hadn't ended the day she had returned home to her family. In early February she went to the Doctor complaining of nausea. At first she thought it had been a stomach bug, or something she had eaten. When it continued she schedule an appointment. She knew that she had missed her monthly periods but figured it was due to the stress she had been under. After the ER physician ran a series of tests, they found that she was several months pregnant. Her friends and family were in disbelief. With her and her parents being strong Catholics, they all agreed that an abortion was not the route to go. The decision was made to go through with the pregnancy, and when the baby was born she could decide whether she would keep the baby or put it up for adoption.

Detective Caldwell still held on to a lot of guilt surrounding the case, but he continued his updates with Mr. and Mrs. Foster.

After the Scarecrow had managed to escape with Michelle, the Foster family had hired a private investigator to help with the case. Caldwell wasn't surprised. Some big shot from Amarillo who had made a name for himself was now working on the case that had seemed to break Detective Caldwell's spirit. The PI had even promised the Foster family that he would be the one to bring Michelle home.

Caldwell had sat alone at night many times, contemplating whether he should walk into the police station and turn in his badge or continue trying to find the one who had beaten him. If he had quit when the kidnapper had asked him to instead of allowing his ego to win, maybe Michelle would be home too. These were the thoughts that haunted him daily.

The shrine of awards that had once covered his office wall was now gone. The twenty-two plus awards could now be found collecting dust in an old shipping container he had rented.

Detective Shawn Peterson was still with the force and had received a promotion. He would stop in frequently to check on Caldwell, and they would talk about the good old days. It never failed that Peterson wanted to hear one of the stories from Caldwell's past. Peterson knew the hurt and embarrassment that Caldwell had felt after losing to the Scarecrow, so he made a point to ask him about the successful career he'd had in an attempt to remind him of all the good he had done.

One Thursday afternoon about 3:00 p.m., Peterson stopped in to visit with Caldwell.

"You had some letters in your office mailbox; I went ahead and grabbed them for you," he said.

"I appreciate it, Shawn. Man, I'm ready for this week to be over with," Caldwell said while scanning through the letters.

He was almost finished when it caught his eye. An envelope with a big smiley face drawn on it.

He knew immediately whom it had to be from. His mind flashed back to seeing the single yellow sticky note at the crime scene with the same smiley face and the message *Maybe next time*. He turned to the wall, where the yellow note had made its way to the Scarecrow shrine. He walked over to the wall and held up the envelope next to the note; the smiley faces were the same.

Not a day had gone by since finding the sticky note the Scarecrow had left behind that he hadn't looked at it and seen the three-worded phrase that had been eating at him for the past few months.

He opened the envelope and pulled out the letter inside. Unfolding it, he read out loud, "Hey there, Detective, still looking for me?"

AUTHOR'S NOTE

I HOPE YOU HAVE enjoyed the journey of Detective Marc Caldwell and his hunt to catch the Scarecrow. Unfortunately the world we live in is not perfect and actual incidents like these occur far more often than they should. On average 90,000 people are missing in the United States at any given time. In 2016 there were over 262,707 females and 232,443 males under the age of twenty-one that were reported missing in the United States alone. Phoenix, Arizona, is currently the kidnapping capital of America, with more incidents than any other city in the world outside of Mexico City. Human sex trafficking is at an all-time high, and many of the people who go missing are believed to have been victims of this criminal industry. I hope to shine a light on the ever-increasing dangers that are imminent for our teens and young adults in the world today. The first forty-eight hours after a person goes missing are the most critical and for children that number drops. Seventy-six percent of abducted children who are murdered are killed within the first three hours after going missing. If someone you know is missing, call 911 or notify the local authorities as quickly as possible; there is no mandatory waiting period to file a missing person's report.